D1563238

Introduction to Business Analytics

Introduction to Business Analytics

Majid Nabavi and David L. Olson

BEP BUSINESS EXPERT PRESS

Introduction to Business Analytics

First published in 2019 by
Business Expert Press, LLC
222 East 46th Street, New York, NY 10017
www.businessexpertpress.com

ISBN-13: 978-1-94944-327-1 (paperback)
ISBN-13: 978-1-94944-328-8 (e-book)

Business Expert Press Big Data and Business Analytics Collection

Collection ISSN: 2333-6749 (print)
Collection ISSN: 2333-6757 (electronic)

Cover and interior design by Exeter Premedia Services Private Ltd., Chennai, India

First edition: 2019

10 9 8 7 6 5 4 3 2 1

Printed in the United States of America.

Abstract

This book is intended to present key concepts related to quantitative analysis in business. It is targeted to business students (both undergraduate and graduate) taking an introductory core course. Business analytics has grown to be a key topic in business curricula, and there is a need for stronger quantitative skills and understanding of fundamental concepts.

Keywords

business analytics; forecasting; hypothesis testing; knowledge management; regression; statistical sampling

Contents

CHAPTER 1

Business Analytics

Business analytics refers to the use of quantitative analysis to support managerial decision making. It is concerned with the process of managerial decision making, as well as the tools used to support it (management science). Information is a valuable asset requiring careful management, to make sure that businesses are able to accomplish their missions, no matter what those might be. In the agricultural domain, the production, processing, and marketing of food to keep us all going involves many participants, although there are a relatively small number of major producers such as ConAgra, ADM, Kellogg's, and so on. These major producers have massive data processing challenges, concerning weather, markets, production of many commodities across the world, and many types of demand. In the retail domain, Wal-Mart and its competitors deal with many products coming from many places, and stock these products in many retail outlets, served by a massive distribution network. Keeping on top of data is crucial to Wal-Mart's success, served by what is probably the world's largest data processing system. Distribution requires a massive transportation network. One element is the airline industry, which has to keep track of many customers seeking to travel from one location to another. Governments also have massive data needs. Providing protection to citizens requires collecting and processing data on airline traffic, shipping, road networks, population movements, economic activity, and risks of nature in the form of weather, volcanic activity, tsunamis, and so on.

Information can be viewed in a variety of ways. You might think of raw data as an initial form that humans need to process into understanding through various stages. But classifying these stages is probably unnecessary—our world today is flooded with data from a variety of forms. For almost centuries, the U.S. government has collected census data (as the

Romans did millennia ago). In the last century, a sophisticated system of economic data collection was developed in the United States, followed by OECD in Europe, and UN data of various types. Businesses also collect data, seeking to gain competitive advantage by understanding what the opportunities are in their markets. Science has been in favor of open data, shared so that humanity as a whole can gain understanding more rapidly. The medical scientific field consists of a complex network of researchers seeking cures to cancer and other evils. The business domain overlaps this scientific endeavor in the form of the pharmaceutical industry, resulting in an interesting dichotomy of interest between open sharing of information for the sake of progress versus intellectual property protection to further pharmaceutical profitability.

There are two major developments in recent years that have revolutionized the field of information. Supply chain networks have evolved, enabling linking a multitude of vendors from practically anywhere across the globe with businesses adept and processing or manufacturing products. Their production expertise can often be applied in many different locations, enabling them to find cheaper labor to make products, transported over a sophisticated distribution network. It is astounding to consider how fruits from Central or South America, grains from Africa as well as the Midwestern U.S., and meats from Australia and Argentina can find their way to our groceries in Europe or the United States. The resulting supply chain networks usually find it worthwhile to be open in sharing data with their supply chain partners, much as keiretsus and chaebols have operated in eastern Asia.

A second major development is the explosion of social media, which has led to linkages of people around the globe. Many countries find far more people using cell phones than landlines, and even places like the United States where landlines have been in place for over 100 years now see most people abandoning the old systems for cheaper and more mobile cell phones. These devices, along with a plethora of other platforms such as smartphones and tablets supported by free access to the World Wide Web, enable people to talk to each other over Facebook and to purchase products from organizations such as Amazon. This has led to masses of data being accessible to businesses to collect and analyze (a business form of Big Data).

Business Decision Making

Science seeks to gain complete understanding of whatever topic is under consideration, identifying the entire system of interacting parts, how they relate to each other and how this leads to outcomes. The field of physics has successfully been able to send rockets (some occupied by humans) to the moon, and more impressively, to return safely. Geology has studied the components of the earth and scientists are able to identify properties useful to growing crops in particular locations, as well as identify likely places for oil discovery or the discovery or rare earth elements. Chemistry has been able to develop combinations of atoms to propel vehicles, to blow things up, and to deliver pills making us feel better. Biology seeks to understand how organisms go through their life cycles.

Science has accomplished a great deal, but not that humans have not gained perfect understanding of anything. The degree of how well bodies of scientific theory can explain natural phenomena varies. In physics and geology, the scientific process has accomplished a great deal. Chemistry has also seen many useful gains, although the interactions of various drugs on humans are far from understood. Biology includes even greater uncertainty, and medical science has a long way to go to master human and other animal systems. When you get to economics and other human behavior, the mysteries deepen.

Business has always involved the interactions of many people. These people make assumptions, to cope with the complexities of their lives. Making assumptions is a necessary part of theory building necessary to surviving everyday life. But many times assumptions are based on false speculation, resulting in incorrect understanding and poor decisions. The contention we propose is that gathering data and measuring what is going on in businesses can lead to better understanding, and consequently, better decision making. This is not expected by any means to be a cure-all. No matter how much we think we know, there will be mistakes in our theories of cause and effect, as well as our understanding what is currently going on. But we have to keep trying.

LaPlace once contended that if he knew the starting conditions, he could calculate how anything would behave. This represents a type of reductionism, which pure scientists often adopt. It is a Newtonian view of strict causality, which implies that if you can't measure and explain, it isn't scientifically understood. This view complies with the idea of determinism, that everything that unfolds in the world is describable by natural law.

This idea is not necessarily wrong, but in the domain of business seems impractical, either due to the complexity involved in our world, or the continual change endemic to natural as well as human activity. Thus it is necessary to view life more flexibly, to understand that systems are complex and change, and that what has happened in a particular context in the past is not necessarily going to be the same in the future. Business has to face changes in laws and regulations, in societal attitudes regarding what is acceptable behavior, and the high levels of uncertainty involved in markets.

Thus there is not "only one best way" in any business decision context. Management is getting things done through people, and whenever you have people involved, you find changes in mood in individuals, and different attitudes across people, and different market behavior for different profiles of customers. Management thus has to combine a scientific-like process of theory verified by observation along with an art of getting along with a wide variety of people. Managerial decision making is the most fundamental function of management, and a very difficult task where demanding stakeholders are never satisfied.

Scientific Method

Science is a process, seeking to carefully study a problem and evolve over time with a complete mathematical description of a system. This seeks to be completely objective, measuring everything accurately and developing theories with no emotional bias. This scientific approach, as we have alluded to before, has served humanity well in many environments. We think it seems to do better when human choice is not involved, as we humans have always reserved the right to change our minds and behavior.

The scientific method can be viewed as a process consisting of the following elements:

- Define the problem (system)
- Collect data

- Develop hypotheses of cause and effect in the interaction of system elements
- Test these hypotheses
- Analyze results
- Refine our mental models or theories of cause and effect

This scientific method has led to impressive understanding of the laws of physics. Astronomers continue to expand our understanding of the universe, through more powerful telescopic tools as well as spectral analysis of elements. Einstein was able to formulate a mathematical expression of the relationship between energy, mass and light. USSR cosmonauts and NASA in the United States were able to send rockets into orbit, and to enable men to walk on the moon.

It does make sense to try to apply this same mindset to business. Businesses are complex collections of individuals with different backgrounds, training, and roles, each with their own set of ambitions and agenda. Thus there will often be differing theories, biased by perceptions of self-interest, among the people in any organization. We expect that those that operate more objectively will prevail (although life doesn't guarantee that), and that businesses will do better if they are guided by leaders seeking to be as scientific as they can be, given that they understand that economic activities are very complex and changeable.

Management Decision Process

Keeping in mind that we don't expect that you can be completely scientific in business, a sound objective approach would be expected to serve businesses better than a chaotic decision making environment that operates at random. Thus an analogy to the scientific method outlined earlier might be:

- Define the decision problem (what products to carry)
- Search for data and information (what demand has been observed in this area)
- Generate alternative actions (gather prospective vendor products and prices)

- Analyze feasible alternatives (consider price, quality, and delivery)
- Select best action (select products and vendors)
- Implement (stock your outlets)

This process provides a means to be as scientific as possible within the confines of the chaos and uncertainty of business. Defining decision problems is often imposed by the job business people have. Getting data is critical. Organizational information systems are designed to provide reports that were expected to provide key information enabling everybody in the organization to do their job. But these reports rarely include everything that matters, so employees have to supplement ERP reports with other information. Observation and talking to people is a good source. But we can also go find other information, on the Web, in libraries, even creating experiments to try to understand the systems we have to deal with. Statistical analysis provides valuable tools to monitor performance.

Generating alternative actions is often a matter of creativity. Part of the job of management is to monitor your responsibilities to identify where action is required. This is hard, because it is human nature to see maybe nine problems for every real problem. Systems often self-correct, and micromanaging can be highly detrimental. Experience is extremely valuable in this context, learning when to take action and when to leave things alone. If action is taken, there are many things that could be done. We will look at models as means to anticipate expected outcomes, or in special circumstances, suggest optimal solutions. They are valuable tools for analysis of alternative actions.

Selecting the action to take should not be surrendered to models. Every model involves assumptions, and the models that appear the most powerful usually involve the most assumptions. Thus human judgment needs to be the final decision maker. Models provide useful input, and means to experiment. But we still live in a world where humans are in charge of computers.

Once action is taken, the results need to be monitored. If you make a decision to raise prices on your product, you need to monitor the impact in demand (which probably will go down, but you won't know by how much until you observe and measure).

Management Science

Management science is the field of study seeking to apply quantitative models to common management decisions. It is a parallel field to operations research, which developed in the engineering field. The modeling tools used are common to both fields. These models allow decision makers to experiment, intending to learn more about their operations.

Management science involves purpose-oriented decision making, following the management decision process we have just outlined. Systems have to be understood, including relationships between various resources available to managers, which they apply to accomplish organizational goals. Management science is a toolbox of quantitative methods available. Decision making units need to understand problems, monitor data, and then select one or more management science methods to try to better understand what to expect.

Table 1.1 outlines one view of the primary tools available from management science.

Table 1.1 Management science techniques

Category	Technique	Example use
Statistics	Measure	Monitor performance
Probabilistic	Queuing	Waiting line performance
	Inventory analysis	EOQ, ROP
	Markov chains	Marketing
Simulation	Monte Carlo	Distributions, system performance
	System simulation	Complex waiting line performance
Optimization	Linear programming	Best solution
	Transportation	Moving things the cheapest way
	Assignment	Assigning tasks the best way
	Nonlinear	Economic models
	Network models	Special cases
	Critical path	Project scheduling
	Dynamic programming	Contingent behavior
	Nonlinear programming	Chance constrained models
Decision theory	Decision trees	Probability
Game theory	Consider actions of others	Competitive environments

Statistics can be viewed as the science of collecting, organizing, analyzing, interpreting, and presenting data. It is a fundamental quantitative set of techniques used to measure things. Almost every input to the other models in Table 1.1 are obtained through some level of statistical analysis. Even when human opinion is used to generate input, the impact should be measured statistically.

There are a number of probabilistic modeling techniques. In production systems, or in service business, waiting lines are commonly encountered. Inventory modeling is a fundamental probabilistic component of operations management, with demand being notoriously probabilistic. Analytical models exist for given sets of assumptions, just as they are in queuing models, but simulation is attractive in that it allows any number of assumptions to be included in models. In production systems, arrival rates may be fairly constant, as in assembly lines. But in service systems, such as bank teller windows, arrival of business tends to be highly variable. The expected performance in terms of waiting time and waiting line length can be predicted through queuing models. Markov chains are another form of probabilistic model, where various states can be occupied by entities, transferring to other states at various rates. Overall equilibrium performance can be predicted through these models.

Simulation is a very useful general field that can be used to model just about any system. This enables realistic models with probability distributions allowable for system entities. Unfortunately, the more reality that is modeled through probabilistic elements, the more difficult it becomes to make sense of the output. Probabilistic models such as queuing work when only a few rigid assumptions are made. Simulation allows the modeler to include as many assumptions as desired.

Optimization is the most powerful type of management science model. The standard is linear programming, where any one objective function can be optimized subject to a set of linear constraints. This has proven highly valuable in many contexts, to include petroleum refinery planning, or factory product mix decision making. The downside is that linear programming generates optimal solutions only if assumptions relative to linear functions and parameter certainty are met. If these assumptions are not appropriate, the resulting linear programming solution can be radically inferior. Linear programming also assumes that continuous variable values are allowed, although refinements in the form of integer or zero-one programming are available if that assumption is not appropriate.

There are many modifications to the basic idea of optimization modeling. Transportation models are a special case of linear programming, where there are sources and destinations, with different costs over each connection. This could be modeled as a linear program, but a transportation algorithm is much more efficient, allowing modeling much larger problems. Assignment models are a special case of transportation algorithms, where the sources and demands are all one.

Network models can be modeled for specific problems such as identifying the shortest path to visit each of a set of locations, or finding a lowest-cost way to connect a network of elements, or maximum flow models seeking to find the highest volume of flow over a network. Critical path models are useful in project management, identifying the earliest finish time schedule for a series of project activities with given durations and predecessor relationships.

Dynamic programming optimizes, but in a sequential form of modeling, enabling dealing with problems that would otherwise involve too many combinations. Nonlinear programming is just like basic linear programming, with nonlinear functions allowed. This is useful in some contexts such as chance constrained modeling, where the assumption of certainty is replaced with statistical distributions. Nonlinear models are harder to optimally solve, but software has become widely available to support it.

Decision theory includes two useful categories of models. Decision trees provide a means to incorporate combinations of decision maker choices with probabilistic outcomes. This broad category of model could also include multiple attribute decision making, to include utility theory, analytic hierarchy process, and other techniques to make selection choices under conditions of trade-offs. Game theory is a class of modeling dealing with competitive situations, considering the actions of others.

Knowledge Management

Knowledge management (KM) is a broad field including identification, acquisition, storage, and retrieval of information to aid decision making.

These four functions are processes of KM. Identification requires focusing on the information important in supporting organizational decision making, selecting the best available measures to support these decisions. Knowledge acquisition involves getting the data providing these measures, which can involve aggregating data from internal systems such as ERP, extracting data from governmental or commercial sources for data external to the organization, and even conducting research to obtain more specific data. Storage is usually an information systems or information technology task, supplemented by individual databases. And what is entered into storage needs to be retrievable.

KM is process oriented, thinking in terms of how knowledge can be acquired, as well as tools to aid decision making. Rothberg and Erickson's (2005) framework defined data as observation, which when put into context becomes information, which in turn can be processed by human understanding to become knowledge. Big data can be a source used to generate insights, innovation, and business value by providing real-time measures of performance, more timely analyses based on more complete data, and can lead to sounder decisions.

Big Data

KM today is characterized by the existence of big data. The advent of i-phones and other hand-held devices has led to an explosion in data. Our culture has become obsessed with sharing many details about ourselves. Some of this self-centered desire to share everything about ourselves with the world has been found useful to many retail organizations. There also is a great deal of useful information generated from e-business activity. Thus we have big data, too massive to store on a single server, too unstructured to fit within standard spreadsheet formats, continuously generated, with little structure (Davenport 2014). This big data explosion has had highly important impact on KM, offering many opportunities to business organizations and to identity thieves.

Three aspects of big data found important are volume, velocity, and variety:

- Volume is an important aspect of KM, as streams of data arrive in real time from cash registers. Large organizations such as Wal-Mart have found it worthwhile to capture this information, aggregate it, providing capability to generate customer profiles to enable real-time marketing opportunities custom tailored to milk the maximum revenue stream from each source. This information can also be used to manage inventories, and to deal with vendors.

- Velocity is important to enable real-time response. One of the most voluminous types of data is the weather data generated by satellites, streamed back to earth-bound computers, which need to process this information and feed useful information to weather reporters throughout the world. Military operations also have high velocity information that needs to be made sense of to enable rapid decisions concerning targeting and other military applications. Retail business also needs to be able to operate in real-time, which requires high-velocity capabilities.
- Variety is important in many applications. Social media generate data useful to retail businesses. This social media data consists of many data formats, to include networks of links, photographic data, movie data, and so on. The medical industry has become a major part of the global economy, with even more complex data formats, to include MRI data, DNA data, and ever-evolving new format types.

The Computer System Perspective

The role of information systems is to provide organizational leadership with an accurate picture of what is going on in their areas of responsibility. Management information systems have evolved to sophisticated enterprise systems, integrating diverse reporting elements to provide comprehensive and systematic reporting. But there has always been an evolutionary aspect to organizational information, with individual elements having their own needs. Within the field of enterprise systems, there are giant firms such as SAP, Oracle, and Infor that provide top-scale support. These are supplemented by a level of commercial systems specializing in areas such as transportation management systems, warehouse management systems, manufacturing execution systems, advanced planning systems, and so on. There will always be new software tools developed and marketed that offer more focused and affordable service to their clients. This includes focused systems that were once referred to as decision support, providing dedicated systems to provide individual decision making entities with access to data, modeling, and reporting tools for specific decision problems.

Among the many computer systems supporting decision making are tools such as Tableau, which provides a useful database by county or zip-code, with demographic data, that can be used to visually or tabular display demand for specific products. These software tools emphasized the visualization aspects of information analysis, providing highly useful marketing support.

The Analytics Perspective

The analytics perspective involves various forms of management science, which has been around since World War II, and in the field of inventory management, longer than that. This includes the need to consider sustainability in this era of global warming, as well as risk management. Davenport (2013) reviewed three eras of analytics. In the first, business intelligence, focused on computer systems such as decision support systems harnessing custom-selected data and models. In the early 21st century, big data generated from Internet and social media provided a second focus. Davenport saw a third era involving a data-enriched environment with online real-time analysis.

The Internet of things provides an additional source of big data. Just as people can communicate through text, e-mail, and other forms of communication, machines communicate with each other. In the health care industry, Fitbits and other personal monitoring devices generate data that could conceivably link to personal physicians. The problem physicians would have coping with this potential flood of data is thought provoking. How people ever survived until 2010 is truly a wonder. Out of massive quantities of data, only a miniscule bit is germane. Of course, signals are sent only when critical limits are reached, but if the system scales up to include the majority of the billions of people inhabiting the earth, it would seem that some means of management of data volume would grow in importance.

Modeling Decision Environments

The point of analytical modeling is to construct an abstraction of a real system capturing the key elements involved, and then solving the resulting model to arrive at a way to improve this real system. Models can take many forms, to include maps, organizational charts, or even physical analogs such as model airplanes. Management science models are mathematical abstractions using variables and functional relationships, a symbolic form of mental model. All models are abstractions of reality, and will always leave out some elements of the reality. The key to success is to capture the essential elements in the model, along with realistic relationships among these elements. This enables experimentation to predict outcomes resulting from system changes. The model will include expected relationships of cause and effect. For instance, a model might include variables for alternative products to manufacture, such as automobile styles. These products would require resources, in terms of labor hours, tons of steel, tons of chrome, tires, and so on. If the modeler knew how each unit of each style of car used up resources, functions could be constructed to measure the hours and tons used up for any given set of variable values, each of which could be constrained to the amount available. Then if a function measuring profit for each style were available (and all of these functions were linear), an optimization model could be solved to identify the feasible combination of number of automobiles by styles identified that would have the maximum profit. Some terms involved are variables (those things you control, like numbers of automobiles by style) and parameters (constants expressing the contribution to each function, as well as constraint limits).

There are a variety of modeling types. Deterministic models have constants, making it easier to model. Linear programming is the classic deterministic modeling type. Most real decisions involve risk, in terms of parameters described by statistical distributions. Examples include waiting line systems, where arrival rates as well as service times are often probabilistic, as well as inventory models with probabilistic demand distributions. Simulation often is very useful to model systems with distributions. Uncertainty situations involve situations where statistically described distributions aren't available. These can be modeled using decision maker opinions of probabilities. Decision trees are applicable for some uncertain environments, as well as simulation. A fourth category of model type involves conflict, or competitive environments. Game theory is applicable in these environments.

Regardless of model type, a modeling process outlined earlier can be applied. Sound modeling practice should begin by assessing the overall decision environment, trying to understand the system of interacting parts and their relationships. This should lead to understanding problem components, to include who is the decision maker, what objectives are important, and what options are available. Then models can be developed by formulating the system mathematically, to include identification of variables, parameters, and functional relationships. This will require trying to express the model in some form you can solve, at the same time that you limit yourself to realistic assumptions. Once a model is constructed, using realistic data, models should be validated in that their results appear to be realistic.

It is important to remember that models are necessarily simplifications of reality. They can be made more complicated, capturing more real details. But that requires more detailed data collection, and more complicated results that may be harder to explain to managers. Modelers should always remember the assumptions included in their models, and that models are only imperfect reflections of expected reality. Nonetheless, they often enable significant improvement in business decision making.

Business analytics is a broad topic. This book focuses on modeling tools, but keep in mind that these are but one part of the overall field. Business analytics includes identifying the specific decisions that need to be made, as well as data that is needed for decision makers to make informed decisions (and that provide sound sources of input for the models we discuss). Thus understanding the business system is probably the most important step in business analytics. Then data needs to be managed. In recent years, most large organizations utilize enterprise resource planning systems heavily, but there are many forms of such systems, and they are not the only source of data. But they do provide useful means to monitor events within organizations. Sound management needs to supplement this source with others, to make sure that decision makers have a complete picture of what is going on, and the impact of their decisions needs to be monitored. If sound data is obtained, models can be highly useful.

CHAPTER 2

Visualization

Sharing data and information is an essential part of academic research and professional operations. Creating a common understanding of the information among analysts, managers, and other stakeholders is a challenge. We can often achieve a common understanding of the data and information by summarizing. Transformation of raw data to processed, compact, and understandable format facilitates communication of the data and a common understanding among different groups. Business analytics refers to the skills, technologies, applications and practices for exploration and investigation of past business performance to gain insight to aid business planning.

Methods of data communication are important, particularly when discussing large quantities of data and your audience are from a diverse background. We can use text, numbers, tables, and a variety of graphs for presenting data. The tool we use must be a good fit to the content of information we present. For example, we use graphs when there is a large number of data points or categories, and details are not as important as the overall trend or share of categories in the data pool. For one or two numbers, or observations that can be summarized in one or two numbers, text will work better.

Use of Graphics to Communicate Data

The primary categories of Excel visualization tools consist of tables, graphs, and charts. We will demonstrate these in turn.

Using data tables for demonstrating data usually asks the reader to focus on cells one at a time. A data table is more useful in a report than in presentation (see Table 2.1). We can however, highlight specific cells, rows, or columns to get more attention. Bold and italic fonts, font colors, and background colors are common methods of highlighting partial data.

Table 2.1 Tabular example

Categories	Jan	Feb	Mar
Appliance	200,947	105,433	199,747
Camera	118,260	19,099	113,147
Computer	22,598	211,161	24,236
Phone	**133,997**	**16,597**	**205,298**
Toys	7,611	7,236	7,850
TV	121,130	235,485	281,983

Table 2.2 Heat graph

Categories	Jan	Feb	Mar
Appliance	200,947	105,433	199,747
Camera	118,260	19,099	113,147
Computer	22,598	211,161	24,236
Phone	133,997	16,597	205,298
Toys	7,611	7,236	7,850
TV	121,130	235,485	281,983

Observe the emphasis on the product category of Phone in Table 2.1 for first quarter sales of a retail outlet.

We can create a **Heat Map** (Table 2.2) of a table by conditional formatting. A heat map applies a spectrum of colors to the background according to the relative position of numbers in the table. The preceding table is a heat map of first quarter sales at eCity.

Darker green and red cells are larger and smaller numbers respectively, and lighter colors in between. These colors help us locate larger and smaller numbers quickly, rather than reading the numbers and comparing them.

A few examples of what we can do with graphs include emphasizing trends over time in a line graph, comparing overall count or percentages of categories in bar/column graphs, comparing relative position of two variables in scatter plots, and presenting shares of categories out of a whole population in a pie chart. Figure 2.1 classifies popular graphs and their applications.

Line charts work best for demonstrating variations of continuous variables along another continuous variable such as a time line. This type

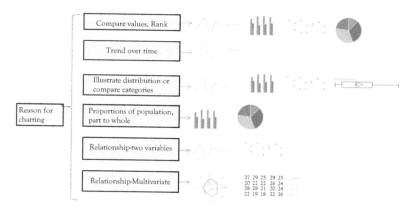

Figure 2.1 *Classification of common graphs*

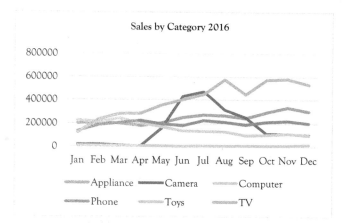

Figure 2.2 *Example line chart*

of chart is not proper for categorical data since the continuity of a line implies continuity of the variable. The following line graph demonstrates total sales of all categories for 12 months. Filtering data may reduce the number of data series (lines) and help focus on one or two categories of interest (Figure 2.2).

Scatter plots are used for showing the relative position of two numeric variables. Two axes, X and Y allow you to observe if a relationship exists between two variables. When increasing the values of one variable, if values of the other variable also increase following a pattern, there is probably a relationship between the two. The following scatter

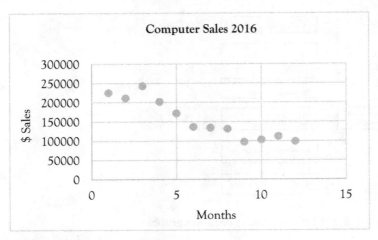

Figure 2.3 Example scatter diagram

plot shows computer sales through 2016. We can observe a relationship between months and sales in this graph. There is an overall downward trend in computer sales through 2016 shown in Figure 2.3.

Bar and Column graphs work well for demonstrating quantities in interval scale. Bar and column graphs emphasize group values to show grouped data in the form of bars or columns, across another variable. Choosing one depends on desired chart orientation: horizontal or vertical. You may consider page orientation and space in a report or slide when choosing between the two. Bars and column scales must include zero, otherwise their relative length will be misleading (Figure 2.4).

First column graph on the top left stacks sales values for all categories during the first five months of 2016. The other three graphs represent exactly the same data in different ways; computer sales during the first five months. The two lower graphs seem to be different in reflecting proportions. Sales in March looks like more than seven times the sales in May in the lower-right side chart, while it is only 1.4 times, as looks in the lower-left chart. The reason for difference is that the right-side chart's vertical axis starts from 160,000, not from zero as in the left-side chart. The minimum zero of all bars is missing in this graph and the height of the chart is about the original size. Everything is in a larger scale. This graph might be misleading for many observers who do not notice the numbers on vertical axis.

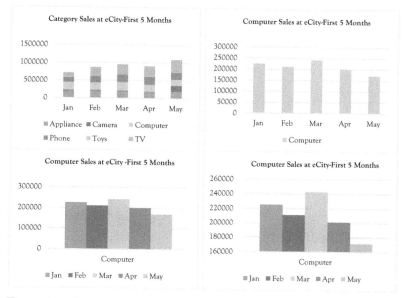

Figure 2.4 Bar and column graphs

Chart Tools

Selecting a chart will activate chart tools including FORMAT and DESIGN tabs. At the same time quick tools will be available on the right side of the chart for adding and removing chart elements, set chart styles, and chart filters to include or exclude partial data (Figure 2.5).

Double clicking chart will open chart task pane which has tools for more control on all chart elements and features. You can open this task pane from chart tools, FORMAT tab, "Current Selection" group, "Format Selection." Task pane tools change according to the chart element you select. After selecting a chart, you can click on each element (chart area, a single dataseries, axis, title, and so on.) and task pane will make tools available to format or change that element.

Figure 2.5 Format and design tabs

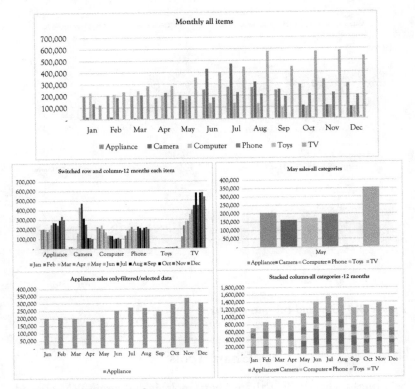

Figure 2.6 Alternate chart panes

Double clicking any chart will open the chart task pane which provides more control over design and formatting of all chart elements. This is a dynamic tool that will customize to format selected chart element. You can select the chart, then click on any element to select it and do changes in task pane. Fill and size, effects, size and proportions, and axis options are four groups of tasks available in task pane.

Use the entire data table in "Column" worksheet in the data file to create a column graph. Switch row and column, select data, and type in titles to create Figure 2.6.

Line Charts

Line charts are good tools for tracking changes over time. Use "Line" worksheet in the data file to create a line chart. Select the entire table and

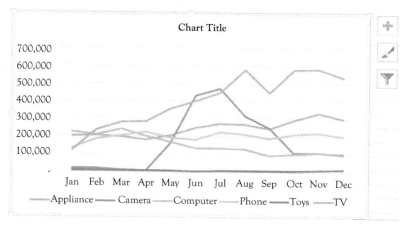

Figure 2.7 Initial line chart

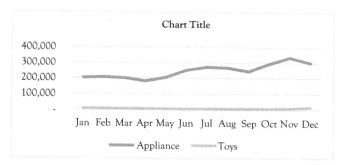

Figure 2.8 Focused selection

insert a line chart under Insert tab, Charts group. This will be a spaghetti chart with too many trends, not the best chart to focus on one or two important points you would like to make. You can use chart tools tabs (Design and Format), that activate when selecting the chart, to select and filter data and do other changes, or the quick tools become visible by selecting the chart—elements, styles, and filters (see Figures 2.7 and 2.8).

Use filter to select Appliance and Toys only. Filter out other categories.

Using Secondary Axis

Toys curve line seems like a flat line along the horizontal axis, due to disparity of numbers between appliances and toys. We can project toys sales

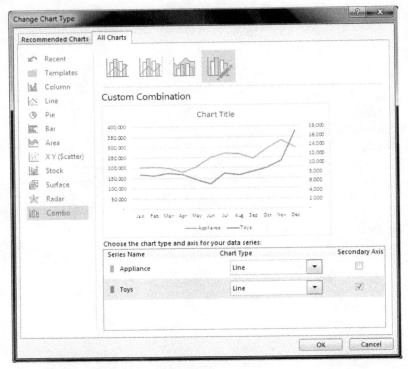

Figure 2.9 Secondary axis selection

on the secondary axis to make variations visible. Right-click on the curve line and from screen menu select "Change series chart type." Check the "Secondary Axis" checkbox in front of Toys and click OK. Now you can see toys sales on the secondary axis, to the right of the chart in Figure 2.9.

Projecting one data series on secondary axis helps with building Pareto charts. These charts use both column and line. Sorted columns represent categories or groups, and line represents cumulative value of those categories.

Pie Charts

Pie charts illustrate portions of a whole in a circle, but have limitations in displaying multiple data series. Use data table in "Pie Chart" worksheet to build a chart. Selecting the entire table and inserting a pie chart will create a chart that uses only the first row of data (Appliance) for 12 months.

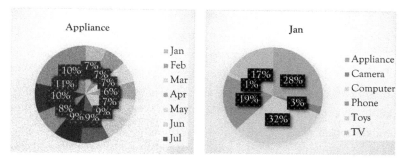

Figure 2.10 Pie charts

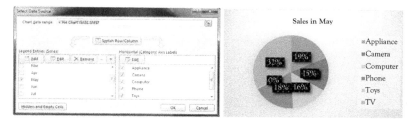

Figure 2.11 Selecting data

Using switch Row/Column from "DESIGN" tab of chart will create a pie chart of all categories in January only (Figure 2.10).

If a pie chart for sales of all categories in May is needed, you can use "Select Data" from "Design" tab and uncheck all months Except May. Selecting/unselecting data series and switching row/column make all charts flexible (Figure 2.11).

Histograms

Histograms are similar to column charts, consisting of columns whose size is proportional to the count of observations in a range (for numeric variables) or to the count of category in sample (for categorical variables). Excel data analysis ToolPak has histogram tool which works for numeric data only. For categorical variables, we need to take extra steps. Histogram worksheet contains demographics and salary information for eCity employees. You can use Excel histogram tool to create histograms for salary and age. Bin ranges are required for running histogram tool. Software needs to "know" the ranges of data we are going to use for slicing the entire data range. Bin range of a numeric variable is a column of numbers marking intervals that start from the smallest value or milestone in the range up to the largest milestone. Salaries are between $20,000 and $100,000 in our data set, so salary bin starts from 20,000 to 90,000 incrementing by 10,000. There is always one bar for "more" that accounts for all observations more than the largest number of the bin. Run histogram tool from data analysis ToolPak, select input range, bin range, output range, and check Chart Output. Click OK to create the histogram. Repeat this process for age. Start with deciding about group intervals for age (Figure 2.12).

Excel 2016 provides histogram tool in Charts group, automatically selecting the bin ranges. You may use this tool for salary data to create the following histogram (Figure 2.13).

Excel histogram tool does not work for non-numeric data. Building a histogram for marital status or gender is not possible by Excel histogram tool. A column chart instead will be our histogram. We need a formula

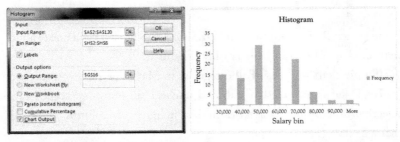

Figure 2.12 Example histogram

Figure 2.13 Excel 2016 histogram tool

to count all levels of the variable. Marital status is a categorical variable with four levels: Single, Married, Divorced, and Widowed. You may put a data filter on your table and easily see unique values of each column when levels of variables are unknown. List these levels in one column and use conditional counting in an adjacent column to count observations of each category.

In the first cell of counting column enter this function and use fill handle to copy it down the column for all levels. List marital status levels in column L and enter this formula in cell M2: =COUNTIF($C$3:$C$120, L2).

This function counts the number of observations in range C3:C120 (Marital status data is in column C) that exactly match cell L2 (Single). Reference to the range is **absolute** (*press F4 when range is selected*). This reference will not change when copying the formula down. Second argument of this function is a **relative reference** to cell L2. This reference will move down when copying the formula to column, so the subsequent cells will count the number of "Married," "Divorced," and "Widowed" (Figure 2.14).

Select the entire range L1:M5, and insert a column chart. This is equivalent to histogram (Figure 2.15).

L	M		L	M
Marital status Bin	**Count**		**Marital status Bin**	**Count**
Single	=COUNTIF($C$2:$C$119,L2)		Single	=COUNTIF($C$2:$C$119,L2)
Married			Married	=COUNTIF($C$2:$C$119,L3)
Divorced			Divorced	=COUNTIF($C$2:$C$119,L4)
Widowed			Widowed	=COUNTIF($C$2:$C$119,L5)

Figure 2.14 Obtaining counts in Excel

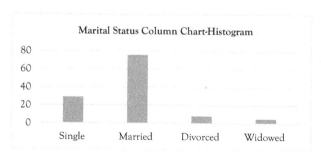

Figure 2.15 Resulting histogram

Conclusions

Data visualization is important as it provides humans an initial understanding of data, which in our contemporary culture is overwhelming. We have demonstrated basic Excel graphical tools, in the high-level categories of graphs, tables, and charts. We also have examined formatting and design tools, and demonstrated basic alternative forms of line charts, pie charts, and histograms. Excel provides some useful basic tools that you as a user can select from to better communicate the story that your data is telling.

CHAPTER 3

Sampling

Sampling is a process of selecting a representative subset of a population for analysis. Sampling and analysis are part of a process to answer research questions. Populations and sampling methods are different, depending on the size and variation of the population, and the question to be answered. For example in a nationwide study of political opinions, people answer questions about their tendency to vote for candidates, or supporting a political party. For potential customers of a new baby stroller, people answer questions about their interest in this product, and their tendency to purchase it. Both studies are nationwide, but the target population is not the same. In the first example, the population is made of all registered voters, and those who plan to register before election day. Younger than 18 and noncitizen residents are not part of the relevant population. Market research for the baby stroller has a population different from potential voters. It is limited to families who expect children. An obvious reason for sampling is that measuring characteristics of the whole population is often not feasible, and in some cases impossible.

Definitions and Concepts

Sampled population is the entire group of people or entities, from which samples are taken. Individuals and entities, **elements** of the population, hold **characteristics** of interest for researchers. By measuring these characteristics, we can estimate population **parameters** such as mean, standard deviation, or **proportion** of groups.

An individual asked about voting in a particular election is a citizen, old enough to vote, and is an element of the sample. Each element has an answer (characteristic) we are interested in. We can estimate proportions of different groups of voters by estimating population parameters from a sample. The population of voters is a **finite population** since it is limited to registered voters.

The population of fuel injection units (elements) in an auto parts manufacturing facility, is all fuel injections manufactured through a specific production line of that facility. These fuel injection units have characteristics that determine their quality. Characteristics can be physical measurements like size and blemishes, or performance outcomes such as the unit functionality or frequency of failure during a test period. We are interested in measurement of these characteristics to use them for estimating population parameters such as average or proportion defectives. These numbers help us understand and improve overall quality of the production system.

While it is ideal to ask everybody about voting, or put every single unit of production through a measurement test, it is not feasible to do so. In most cases, costs of examining the entire population are prohibitive. Some populations like the list of households in the country, change every day. Keeping track of all households all the time is not feasible either. We use a **sampling frame** which is the pool of elements in a population we can sample. Populations like registered voters are **finite**. There is a known list of potential voters. In each state, county, and city we have a known number of people in this pool. Randomly selecting elements of this population is different from the population of fuel injection units, which is **infinite**. The production of units continues to add new elements. We sample only those elements produced during a specific period.

Representative samples can provide a good estimate of population parameters. There are different methods of sampling depending on the nature of the population and characteristics of interest.

Simple random sample is a method of randomly selecting elements given that each element has equal chance of being chosen, and expected characteristics of elements do not have different subsets associated with their other characteristics. An example of this method is randomly selecting 500 individuals of a particular ethnicity for medical research. This method is used when we are not aware of other differences among the group. Having more data about the population may encourage using a different method of sampling.

Stratified random sampling is used when the population has subgroups. These subgroups have a meaningful effect on the value of characteristics we measure. In our example of voters, if there is an expected difference between the tendencies of voters in one state vs. another, we need to consider the proportion of these subgroups in our sample. Sampling for demographics or student opinion about a topic at college of business should include the same proportion of finance, accounting, supply chain management, and other majors, as the population of students of the college.

Random sampling is a process in which we select elements from an infinite population. Random sampling is used when simple random sampling is not possible. One example is a very large population in which tracking all elements in not feasible. Another example is an ongoing process, manufacturing or service, which regularly produces new elements. Developing a frame and taking a representative simple random sample is not possible in this situation. Random sampling is similar to simple random sampling. The difference is that not all elements have equal chance of being chosen.

Systematic sampling is a method in which choosing elements starts from a random point or a specific time and continues at equal intervals. This can be a time (i.e., every hour) or one out of a given number of elements in sequence (i.e., every 200th unit). The interval can be calculated by dividing the population size by the desired sample size. If daily production is 10,000 units and we plan for a sample size of 50, every 200th unit on production line is sampled.

Confidence Level: In quality control process, we consider a level of confidence (i.e., 95%) for our results. Assuming a normal distribution of observations, for a 95% confidence level there is $\alpha = 5\%$ probability of error (see Figure 3.1). We assign $\alpha/2 = 2.5\%$ of this probability to the upper (right), and 2.5% to the lower (left) tail of distribution. Confidence

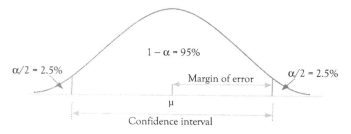

Figure 3.1 Confidence interval in a normal distribution

interval is the area under the curve containing 95% of the space. Margin of error is the distance between the mean and each area of error.

A margin of error equal to 3 standard deviations is a popular limit for control charts, which translates to 99.74% confidence.

Sample size is determined before we start sampling. There are multiple methods for determining sample size. Since our sample mean ($\bar{x}$) is not identical to population mean (μ), we consider the difference of the two as sampling error (E). Standard error of the sample is also determined by dividing the standard deviation of population (σ) by square root of sample size:

$$\sigma_{\bar{x}} = \left(\sigma / \sqrt{n} \right)$$

We have the following relationship between margin of error, confidence level, population standard deviation, and the sample size:

$$E = |\mu - \bar{x}| = Z_{a/2} \, \sigma / \sqrt{n}$$

Solving for sample size "n":

$$n = \left(\frac{Z_{a/2} \cdot \sigma}{E} \right)^2$$

We **subgroup** samples by adding up or averaging characteristics' measurements on elements of our samples.

Quality Control Sampling

Quality control charts are demonstration of characteristics measured on samples, and their confidence intervals. In these visual representation of samples we can easily distinguish the trends, variations, and if there are samples with unacceptable characteristics. These diagnostic steps indicate the presence of potential or existing problems in process. There might be a large difference between output parameters such as average size, and the target value, or too much variation in output.

Two types of characteristics are measured in quality control; **variables** and **attributes**. **Continuous** numbers measures **variables** such as time, weight, length, and volume. **Attributes** like number of defects in a lot, number of blemishes on a car, and number of failures through a 100-hour test of a unit, are measured by **discrete** values. These measurements follow different distributions. Control charts used for demonstrating the position of samples relative to control limits, vary based on these distributions. We introduce a few popular control charts in this chapter.

Average and Range Control Charts

Using continuous numbers for measuring a variable provides more detail information comparing to discrete values and measuring attributes. In variable measurement, each sample includes a number of elements. Using characteristics of interest measured in these elements, we can calculate two important parameters for each sample; mean and range. Means of samples are data points for developing **average chart**. We can observe this chart for indication of mean variations, and if the process works to produce elements with expected characteristics. Sample ranges are difference of the maximum and minimum measurement for characteristic of interest. Ranges are data points for **range chart**, which demonstrates the extent of variations in measurements of each sample.

Upper and lower control limits for average chart are developed based on the overall mean of sample means ($\bar{\bar{X}}$), and the desired confidence level (see Figure 3.2). We will establish confidence interval within 3 standard deviations from the overall mean. A control chart for average of

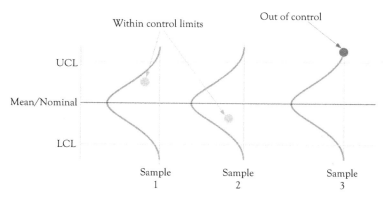

Figure 3.2 Control limits

samples has a horizontal line representing the overall average, or a given target value for the characteristic of interest, as its centerline. This chart has upper and lower control limits, at a distance of 3 standard errors above and below the mean line. Researchers project the average value of each sample on this chart. For an **"in control"** process, all these projections are between the upper and lower control limits. Any point beyond the two control limits indicates the process is **"out of control."**

Formulas for average chart upper and lower control limits:

$$\text{Average Chart Upper Control Limit: } UCL_x = \bar{\bar{X}} + Z_{a/2}\frac{\sigma}{\sqrt{n}}$$

$$\text{Average Chart Lower Control Limit: } LCL_x = \bar{\bar{X}} - Z_{a/2}\frac{\sigma}{\sqrt{n}}$$

Note that these formulas divide the standard deviation by the square root of n—which is appropriate for the average of all observations. However, batching is different—the variance of batch averages is NOT divided by the square root of n—the batching will take care of that.

In range charts, we have only one observation as "range" for each sample. The formulas for upper and lower control limits of range chart simplify as the following:

$$\text{Range Chart Upper Control Limit: } UCL_R = \bar{R} + Z_{a/2}\sigma$$

$$\text{Range Chart Lower Control Limit: } LCL_R = \bar{R} - Z_{a/2}\sigma$$

Standard deviation used in range chart formula is the standard deviation of sample ranges.

In the example data file (extract shown in Table 3.1), we have recordings of samples taken from a steel forging production line. Steel bars made for a designed length. Quality control person takes samples and measure their length every hour, starting 8:30 a.m., followed by seven other samples through 3:30 p.m. There are four machines; A, B, C, and D. Four operators, Liam, Mike, Jacob, and Luke work on these machines. A sampling plan is to take one sample from each machine at every

Table 3.1 *Extract of control sampling data*

	A	B	C	D	E
1	Day	Sample	Length	Machine	Operator
2	1	8:30	2.77	A	Liam
3	1	8:30	2.71	B	Mike
4	1	8:30	2.79	C	Jacob
5	1	8:30	2.83	D	Luke
6	1	9:30	2.73	A	Mike
7	1	9:30	2.77	B	Jacob
8	1	9:30	2.84	C	Luke
9	1	9:30	2.78	D	Liam
10	1	10:30	2.8	A	Jacob

sampling time. Each bar is measured and logged, along with the day of the sampling, sampling time, the machine, and the operator working on that machine at that time. We have eight samples per day, each including four elements (bars), for a total of 32 bars a day. Sampling records for 20 days, records of 640 bars are available.

We are interested in overall performance of the production process. Consistency of the characteristic (length) is our priority. Length is a variable, so we will develop a pair of average and range charts.

We can subgroup elements in different ways. Average and range of sample measurements in each "day," or each "sampling time" are two different ways of subgrouping. We will start with subgrouping by day.

Use "Bar_Defects" worksheet. Insert column headers "Date," "Average_day," and "Range_day" in the first row of columns G, H, and I. Column "Day" requires a sequence of 1 to 20. Column "Average_Day" lists averages of measurements for all days. You can create this list by using the following formula in cell H2, and copying it through range H2:H21. This formula adds up lengths grouped by day, and divides the result by 32, the sample size. All absolute and relative cell references properly work to return the average length of all samples for each day:

=SUMIF($A$2:$A$641, G2,$C$2:$C$641)/32

Another way of calculating average by group is to store the data in a database and run a query for average of lengths, grouped by day. An SQL script for calculating average daily measurements from data stored in Access table named "Defects_Data" is:

```
SELECT Day, AVG(Length) AS Average_Length
FROM Defects_Data
GROUP BY Day;
```

The following query on the same table returns the range of measurements for each day:

```
SELECT Day, (MAX(Length) – MIN(Length)) AS Range
FROM Defects_Data
GROUP BY Day;
```
Copy results into your Excel worksheet (Table 3.2).

Use the list of days, averages, and ranges in columns G, H, and I for calculating control limits and creating charts. The following formulas calculate upper and lower control limits for average chart. Use the upper and lower control limit formulas for average chart:

$$UCL_x = \bar{\bar{X}} + Z_{a/2}\frac{\sigma}{\sqrt{n}} = 2.759 + Z_{a/2}\left(\frac{0.0829}{\sqrt{32}}\right)$$ If a Z of 3 were used, this=2.802

$$LCL_x = \bar{\bar{X}} - Z_{a/2}\frac{\sigma}{\sqrt{n}} = 2.759 - Z_{a/2}\left(\frac{0.0829}{\sqrt{32}}\right)$$ If a Z of 3 were used, this=2.715

Table 3.2 Results copied

G	H	I
Day	Average_day	Range_day
1	2.765625	0.25
2	2.7346875	0.26
3	2.759375	0.28

Upper and lower control limits for range chart are calculated by the following formulas:

$\text{UCL}_R = \bar{R} + Z_{a/2} \cdot \sigma = 0.311 + Z_{a/2}(0.0574)$ If a Z of 3 were used, this=0.483

$\text{LCL}_R = \bar{R} - Z_{a/2} \cdot \sigma = 0.311 - Z_{a/2}(0.0574)$ If a Z of 3 were used, this=0.139

Use Excel function STDEV.S( ) for calculating the standard deviation of length measurements. Figure 3.3 demonstrates complete control limit calculations in Excel (this example uses a Z of 3—you can replace that with the appropriate normal distribution Z score for $\alpha/2$ to obtain limits at specified probabilities in assignments):

Build the Average Chart: average chart has five components:

1. Mean line: a straight line projecting calculated average of the measurements
2. Upper control limit: a straight line demonstrating the upper control limit
3. Lower control limit: a straight line demonstrating the lower control limit
4. Observations: average points calculated. We demonstrate these points as dots on the chart
5. Subgroup markers: mark the values of subgroups on the horizontal axis of chart

	P	Q	R	S
6		StDev (Avg)	StDev(Range)	sample size
7		=STDEV.S(C2:C641)	=STDEV.S(I2:I21)	32
8		=STDEV.S(H2:H21)		
9		=Q7/SQRT(S7)	=AVERAGE(H2:H21)	
10		$\bar{\bar{x}}$	R	
11	UCL	=R9+3*Q9	=AVERAGE($I$2:$I$21)+3*$R$7	
12	LCL	=R9-3*Q9	=AVERAGE($I$2:$I$21)-3*$R$7	

Figure 3.3 Control chart calculation in Excel

Table 3.3 Excel input to generate average charts

	A	B	C	D	E
1		Average_day	Overall Average	UCL$_x$	LCL$_x$
2	1	2.765625	2.758546875	2.802145	2.714949
3	2	2.7346875	2.758546875	2.802145	2.714949
4	3	2.759375	2.758546875	2.802145	2.714949
5	4	2.7646875	2.758546875	2.802145	2.714949
6	5	2.7278125	2.758546875	2.802145	2.714949
7	6	2.746875	2.758546875	2.802145	2.714949

Build charts by copying values in five columns (Table 3.3):

> Column A: Days, listed 1 to 20 and used for marking subgroups. This column does not have a header.
> Column B: Average measurements for all days.
> Column C: Overall average ($\bar{\bar{X}}$).
> Column D: Upper Control Limit.
> Column E: Lower Control Limit.
> All values in each column of C, D, and E are the same, creating a straight horizontal line.

Select the entire data range and insert a line chart. The resulting average chart includes upper and lower control limits, the mean line, subgroup markers on the horizontal axis, and projection of daily averages as a line. We can identify the observations where average is beyond the control limits (see Figure 3.4).

For illustrating averages as points, do the following steps:

- Select Average_day line and right click on the selected line
- Screen menu pops up. Select "Change Series Chart Type"
- "Change Chart Type" dialog box opens. Change "Average_day" type from line to scatter
- Click OK

Figure 3.5 demonstrates the sequence of changing one data series chart type.

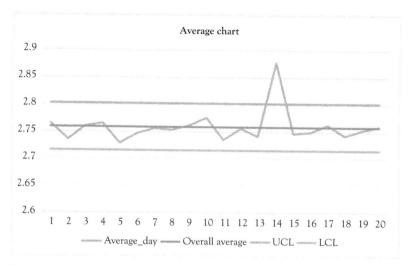

Figure 3.4 Average chart control limit plot

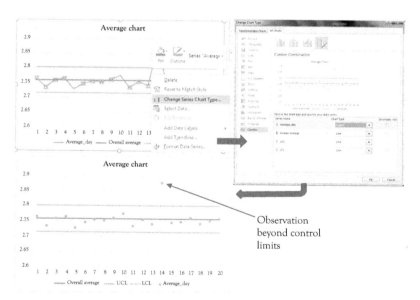

Figure 3.5 Control limit interpretation

Range Chart: create a table similar to the one used for average chart. List of days in the first column make subgroup markers. Second column lists the ranges of measurements for all days. Third column fills with average of ranges, values in the second column. Fourth and fifth column are

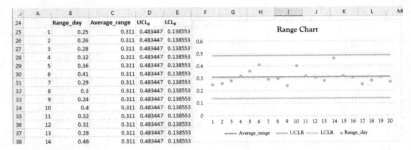

Figure 3.6 Range chart plot

upper and lower control limits. Insert a line chart on this data and change "Range_day" data series chart type to Scatter, similar to the change in average chart. The range chart in Figure 3.6 shows no out of control observation:

Control Charts for Attributes (C-Charts)

In quality control, we do not always measure a variable. Tracking all details may not be required or not feasible in all cases. For example when controlling for blemishes on car bodies after painting, or imperfections of carpets out of a production line, we do not need to measure the exact size or color of the spots. Counting and logging the number of nonconformities are practical solutions in these cases. Size, shape, and color of these blemishes may not play a significant role in quality control decisions. The important data we need is the frequency of nonconformities.

We discuss two methods for recording and analyzing nonconformities. The first method is counting the number of nonconformities in each element of the sample. We use C-Chart in this method. The second method sets acceptance criteria for elements. Any element conforming to all expected specifications is acceptable, otherwise considered a defect. Proportion of defects in samples can determine how the production process conforms to specifications. P-Chart is used in this method.

C-Charts: Counting the number of quality problems in each sampled unit or time interval is one of the inspection methods. Examples include inspection of 50-yard carpet roles, 10-mile segments of a highway checked for maintenance spots, and inspection of one element, typically a complex product sampled from a production line. A car may have many problems right out of the assembly line, but the manufacturer tries to fix these problems rather than calling it a defect and scraping it. A roll of carpet may have a variety of problems such as discolored spots and pieces of fabric that do not match the designed pattern. Frequency of these problems may downgrade the carpet, but it still holds some value. Tracking these problems is valuable for improving the production process. C-Charts are useful for assessing overall performance of a process and its stability. They are a tool for comparing the system performance before and after a process change.

Finding each instance of imperfection in a time interval or in each element sampled, is an **event**. Frequency of events follows a **Poisson** distribution. C-Chart is used for tracking and demonstrating frequency of defects on more complex, and usually more expensive products and services that cannot be simply ruled out as defective. Similar to other control charts, C-Chart projects the sampling results around a centerline. Upper and lower control limit formulas establish limits at +/- 3 standard deviations around the mean. In a Poisson distribution, mean and variance are equal:

$\overline{c}$ = Average number of events in one interval=Variance of the number of events in intervals.

Given "C_i" is the number of defects counted for the ith element and "k" represents the number of elements in our sample:

$$\overline{c} = \frac{\sum_{i=1}^{k} c_i}{k}$$

Upper and lower control limit formulas for a C-Chart are:

$$\mathrm{UCL}_C = \overline{c} + Z_{a/2}\sqrt{\overline{c}}$$

$$\mathrm{LCL}_C = \overline{c} - Z_{a/2}\sqrt{\overline{c}}$$

In "C-Chart" worksheet, we have an example data set of 50 cars inspected for cosmetic, electrical, and mechanical problems. Each car received a sample number, used for a log of the number of problems

Table 3.4 Excel data for C-chart

▲	A	B	C	D	E
1		Observed Defects	Average	UCL_c	LCL_c
2	1		5 =AVERAGE($B$2:$B$51)	=C2+1.645*SQRT(C2)	=C2-1.645*SQRT(C2)
3	2		3 =AVERAGE($B$2:$B$51)	=C3+1.645*SQRT(C3)	=C3-1.645*SQRT(C3)
4	3		5 =AVERAGE($B$2:$B$51)	=C4+1.645*SQRT(C4)	=C4-1.645*SQRT(C4)
5					
6	7(1-0.9)		1.644853627		

observed. In this sampling we track the number of problems regardless of size, type, intensity, or effect on the status of that element. Calculating average number of defects is the first step for creating a C-Chart for this sample. If we want 90% control limits, $Z_{a/2}$ =1.645. We can plug in the calculated average to upper and lower control limit formulas:

$$\text{UCL}_C = 4 + Z_{a/2}\sqrt{4} = 7.29$$

$$\text{LCL}_C = 4 - Z_{a/2}\sqrt{4} = 0.71$$

Should the lower control limit come out to be a negative number, use zero instead. Table 3.4 demonstrates formulas in Excel. The only change we need is substituting all results in column "E" with zero and inserting a line chart. Change chart type for data series "Observed Defects" to scatter.

Probability Control Charts (P-Charts)

We can inspect elements of samples and count them as acceptable or defective based on their conformance to expected specifications (**P-charts**). Consider finding a defective element as **success** for the process of inspection. **Failure** to find a nonconformity results in element passing the test as acceptable. This is a Bernoulli process. We try each element in sample and mark it as success or failure (pass or found a problem). Probability of "success," finding a nonconformity, follows a binomial distribution. We have the sample size and percentage of defective elements, the two key factors for calculating the mean and standard deviation of a binomial distribution. Data collected from multiple samples can provide enough information to develop the control limits and project each sample's percentage defective. The mean and standard deviation of binomial distribution formulas are:

$$\bar{P} = \frac{\sum_{i=1}^{K} n_i p_i}{\sum_{i=1}^{K} n_i}$$

$$\sigma_p = \sqrt{\frac{\bar{p}(1-\bar{p})}{\bar{n}}}$$

In these formulas:

n_i = Sample size (may be constant or vary for different samples)

$\bar{n}$ = Average sample size

P_i = proportion nonconformity (defective) of sample

$\bar{p}$ = Average proportion defective

σ_p = standard deviation of nonconformities

Upper and lower control limit formulas:

$$\text{UCL}_p = \bar{p} + Z_{a/2}\sqrt{\frac{\bar{p}(1-\bar{p})}{\bar{n}}}$$

$$\text{LCL}_p = \bar{p} - Z_{a/2}\sqrt{\frac{\bar{p}(1-\bar{p})}{\bar{n}}}$$

In Excel exercise file "P-Chart" worksheet, we have records of eCity online customer orders processed at the central warehouse. One hundred orders from each week sampled and inspected for errors during the past 25 weeks. Sample sizes listed in column "B" and number of orders found to be nonconforming in column "C." In this case, we do not have a list or type of problems in customer order processing. All we know is the sample size and number of nonconforming orders. We can calculate the proportion of these nonconformities, then the average proportion of observations in cell "F2" with this formula:

=SUM(C2:C26)/SUM(B2:B26)

If $\bar{p}$ were 0.3 and n were 25, upper and lower control limit formulas at a 90% confidence level would be:

=0.3+1.645×SQRT(0.3×(1-0.3)/25)=0.451

$$=0.3-1.645 \times SQRT(0.3 \times (1-0.3)/25)=0.149$$

Lower control limits could turn out to be greater than one or negative. In such cases, set the limit to one or zero, since we cannot have probabilities outside these values.

Conclusions

Control charts are a fundamental tool for quality control. From the operations management perspective, this is an important tool that has been used for average, range, count, and probability contexts, each demonstrated in this chapter. Probably more fundamental is the concept of probability distribution upon which control charts rely. Quality data very often finds that variance of output is normally distributed. That is not the only possible distribution, but is the assumption made in the formulas used in this chapter. The key point is that you can specify any probability level, with half of the error expected above and below the confidence limits you generate (because normally distributed data is symmetric).

CHAPTER 4

Hypothesis Testing

A hypothesis is a statement about a phenomenon, trying to explain a population parameter or effect of a process when we have limited information about that population or process. A representative sample is used for observation and testing. An inference then made about the population, based on the test results. Increasing productivity after implementing a new benefits plan, treatment effect of a new medication, environmental ramifications of a chemical production plant, and using new technologies for learning, are examples where we state a hypothesis about population or process based on limited observations. Hypothesis testing is a process of statement, determining decision criteria, data collection and computing statistics, and finally making an inference. An example of the effect of a training program for customer service agents at a helpdesk can well explain hypothesis testing process. After each call, customers receive a short survey to rate the service on four criteria using a scale of one (extremely dissatisfied) to five (extremely satisfied). The criteria include timeliness of the service, courtesy of the agent, level of information offered to the customer, and overall satisfaction about the service. Total scores of a survey vary between minimum possible score of four, and maximum of 20. We will understand the results of this new training program by comparing the mean customer rating of agents who did go through the training, with those who have not yet started the program. This will be a test of independent samples. Another way of testing the effect of training program is to compare customer ratings before and after the training for the same group of employees. This will be a Z test for two samples we will explain later.

Hypothesis Testing Process

The following steps will state and test our hypothesis testing process:

Step 1. Hypothesis statement: we always state two hypotheses for each experiment. **Alternative hypothesis (H$_a$)** explains our understanding of the existing difference, or a difference created due to effect of a treatment. In case of training program, we expect the mean of customer satisfaction to increase after training. **Null hypothesis (H$_0$)** on the other hand is a negation of alternative hypothesis. H$_0$ is always about no difference of the population statistic before and after the treatment, no effect of treatment, or no relationship of variables. The formal statement of hypothesis is:

H$_a$: Employee training program will increase customer satisfaction. After training program mean customer rating score is higher than before the training.

H$_a$: $\mu > \mu_0$

H$_0$: Employee training program has no effect on customer satisfaction. Mean customer rating score will not be higher after training program. (It might be about the same or even lower than the mean of scores before training. Any observed difference is due to sampling error).

H$_0$: $\mu \leq \mu_0$

This hypothesis statement leads to a one-tail test, since it identifies a direction of change. A hypothesis that does not refer to the direction of change needs a two-tail test. This type of hypothesis will be introduced later in this chapter.

Step 2. Criteria of decision: The average customer rating is 11.8 and standard deviation of scores is four. To compare mean scores observed after training with the current population mean, we will use the null hypothesis statement as expected sample statistics. If the null hypothesis is true, sample means must be around 11.8. Monotone increasing or decreasing values will not change the shape of the distribution, nor its spread. So if distribution of customer rating is normal, it will still be normal after the training, and standard deviation also will be the same as it was before training. We will use sample mean as decision criterion. This mean should be significantly different from the population mean to show a significant difference due to training. Assuming normal distribution and equal spread of sample and population, a probability boundary is required for the test. 95 percent confidence level is a common boundary, and is used in this example. Figure 4.1 demonstrates a normally distributed population with a shaded area in right tail, representing the upper five percent area under the curve. We call this value alpha level ($\alpha = 0.05$), and shaded area is the critical region. Center of the distribution represents population mean, 11.8. Extremely high means of samples that are significantly different from the current population mean will be in critical region, the shaded area. We can find the Z-score of the 95 percent boundary from a standard normal distribution table as 1.64, or calculate it in Excel using NORM.INV( ) function:

=NORM.INV(0.95,0,1)

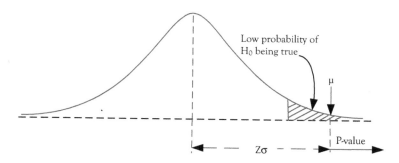

Figure 4.1(a) One tail (upper tail) test of mean. Sample mean is in critical region

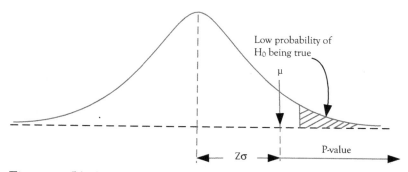

Figure 4.1(b) One tail (upper tail) test of mean. Sample mean is not in critical region

Any Z score of sample means greater than the critical value of 1.64 indicate significant difference of the mean of that sample from the current population mean.

Similarly, when alpha level is 1 percent for a one-tail test, the Z score of the 99 percent boundary is 2.33. Any sample mean Z score larger than 2.33 indicates significant difference of the sample mean from population mean.

Step 3. Observations and sample statistics: data collection for an experiment starts after hypothesis statement and determining decision criteria. We may also have samples taken before stating the hypothesis, but sample information should not introduce bias in hypothesis statement. At this step, we summarize sample data and compute the statistics required for the test. This example is about difference of means for a normally distributed population, with known standard deviation. A Z-test can determine the location of sample statistic relative to the population statistic. Z score formula is:

$$Z = \frac{\bar{X} - \mu}{\sigma_{\bar{X}}}$$

In which:
$\bar{X}$ = Sample mean
μ = hypothesized population mean
$\sigma_{\bar{X}} = \frac{\sigma}{\sqrt{n}}$ = Standard error of the sample
σ = standard deviation of the population
n = sample size

Step 4. Making a decision: The goal of all tests is to reject the null hypothesis. In this example the H_0 states, there is no significant difference between the mean customer satisfaction scores after training, and the current mean of rating. In our example data sample of ratings for 40 employees, the average is calculated as 13.3. Hypothesized mean and standard deviation of the population are 11.8 and 4 respectively. The Z score is calculated as:

$$Z = \frac{13.3 - 11.8}{4 / \sqrt{40}} = 2.37$$

This Z score is greater than the critical boundary Z score of 1.64. Sample mean is within the critical region and there is extremely low probability that a sample from the same population falls within this region. Based on this observation we can reject the null hypothesis and state that the training program significantly increased customer satisfaction.

Figure 4.1(a) and (b) demonstrate sample means within and out of the critical region respectively. Area under the curve beyond the sample statistic (mean) to the right tail, represent **P-value** of the test. This value is an indicator of the significance of this test. P-value of the test must be smaller than the critical boundary (5 percent) in order to reject the null hypothesis. Smaller p-values provide more significant support for rejecting the H_0. We can find the p-value of this test for calculated Z score of 2.37 from a standard normal distribution table, or calculate it in Excel using the following formula:

$$= 1- NORM.S.DIST(2.37,TRUE) = 0.008894$$

NORM.S.DIST( ) function calculates the cumulative probability under a standard normal distribution curve, given the Z score. The formula subtracts this value from 1, the entire area under the curve, to compute the area under the right tail, which is the P-value of this test. This number is the probability that we reject the H_0 while it is true.

Tests of Means

There are parametric and nonparametric tests of mean for two or more samples. Parametric tests are developed for parametric data, making assumptions including normal distribution of population under study. Nonparametric tests are used for both parametric and nonparametric data, and do not have the assumptions of parametric tests including normal distributions. In this section, we explain parametric tests of means for less than three samples.

Z Test for Independent Samples

The test explained through the hypothesis testing example is a Z test for independent samples. This test of means is used when the population

	A	B	C	D	E
1	Employee	Rating			
2	1	9		Mean	=AVERAGE(B2:B41)
3	2	13		Z	=(E2-11.8)/(4/SQRT(40))
4	3	11		P-value	=1- NORM.S.DIST(2.37,TRUE)
5	4	8			
6	5	16			

Figure 4.2 *Computing mean, Z score, and P-value of the Z-test for an independent sample in Excel*

mean and standard deviation are known, and researchers try to detect the effect of a factor on sample means. Use the data set provided in this chapter data file, "Z-test UT" worksheet. Customer ratings for 40 employees after training program are listed in range B2:B41. Enter the formulas demonstrated in cells E2, E3, and E4 of Figure 4.2 to compute the mean, Z score, and p-value of the Z test.

Two-Sample Z Test

Sometimes the research involves comparing two samples with a null hypothesis of equal means. As a two-sample Z test example, we compare mean customer ratings of 40 employees before training and a sample of 40 who have already completed training. Large sample size allows us to use the sample variance as known variance in test of means. Data for two samples is in "Paired Z" worksheet of the data file. Use Excel function VAR.S( ) for computing variance of each range. Excel data analysis Toolpak includes a two-sample Z test tool. The Z test dialog box requires two data ranges and their calculated variances, as well as the hypothesized mean difference. The null hypothesis for this one-tail test states no difference between the means. We use zero as hypothesized difference of means. The default alpha level is 0.05 in this tool. We can change or use the same level. Results are available after selecting the output range and clicking OK. While critical boundary Z score of a one tail test with alpha level of 0.05 is 1.64, the test outcome shows a Z score of −5.249 and a very small P-value. This outcome indicates significant difference between the means of two samples, indicating significant difference made by training program (Figure 4.3).

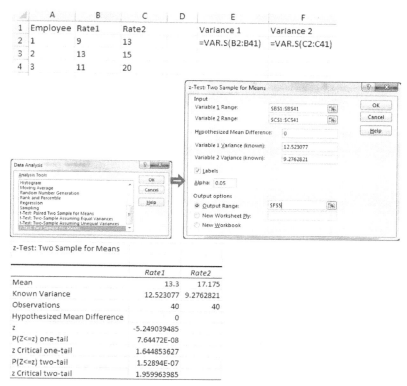

	A	B	C	D	E	F
1	Employee	Rate1	Rate2		Variance 1	Variance 2
2	1	9	13		=VAR.S(B2:B41)	=VAR.S(C2:C41)
3	2	13	15			
4	3	11	20			

z-Test: Two Sample for Means

	Rate1	Rate2
Mean	13.3	17.175
Known Variance	12.523077	9.2762821
Observations	40	40
Hypothesized Mean Difference	0	
z	-5.249039485	
P(Z<=z) one-tail	7.64472E-08	
z Critical one-tail	1.644853627	
P(Z<=z) two-tail	1.52894E-07	
z Critical two-tail	1.959963985	

Figure 4.3 Two-sample Z test in Excel

T-Test

When comparing the means of two samples and the standard deviation of population is not known we use t-test. For samples taken from a normally distributed population, t is a continuous distribution of location of sample means relative to the population mean. We use estimated standard error of the sample to substitute for unknown standard deviation of the population. t value is a substitute of Z score.

Sample variance is the ratio of sum of squared deviations from the mean (SS):

$$\text{Sample variance} = S^2 = \frac{ss}{n-1} = \frac{ss}{df}$$

$$\text{Sample Standard deviation} = S = \sqrt{\frac{ss}{n-1}} = \sqrt{\frac{ss}{df}}$$

$$\text{Standard error} = \sigma_{\bar{x}} = \frac{\sigma}{\sqrt{n}} = \sqrt{\frac{\sigma^2}{n}}$$

$$\text{Estimate of standard error} = S_{\bar{x}} = \frac{s}{\sqrt{n}} = \sqrt{\frac{s^2}{n}}$$

Computing "t" value is similar to Z score, by substituting the population standard deviation with estimated standard error of the sample:

$$t = \frac{\bar{X} - \mu}{s_{\bar{x}}}$$

Excel analysis Toolpak has two sample t-test tools for paired samples, as well as different assumptions of equal and unequal variances. Figure 4.4 demonstrates a t-test of two samples assuming unequal variances. We use the same data set of two customer rating samples for two groups, with and without training. When doing a test of means the null hypothesis is no difference of means, so we enter zero as hypothesized mean difference. The results show a critical t statistic value of 1.665 for one tail test. Absolute value of the calculated t statistic (−5.249) is much larger than the critical value which rejects the null hypothesis of equal means. The p-value of the one tail test is very small relative to alpha level of 0.05. In case we are not sure about the direction of changes due to effect of the factor we are testing, a two-tail test is appropriate. Excel t-test returns values for two-tail test too. Critical t value for two-tail test is 1.99, still smaller than the absolute value of the calculated t for this test.

t-Test: Two-Sample Assuming Equal Variances

Input		
Variable 1 Range:	$B$1:$B$41	
Variable 2 Range:	$C$1:$C$41	
Hypothesized Mean Difference:	0	
☑ Labels		
Alpha:	0.05	
Output options		
◉ Output Range:	$J$3	
○ New Worksheet Ply:		
○ New Workbook		

t-Test: Two-Sample Assuming Unequal Variances

	Rate1	Rate2
Mean	13.3	17.175
Variance	12.52307692	9.276282051
Observations	40	40
Hypothesized Mean Difference	0	
df	76	
t Stat	-5.249039501	
P(T<=t) one-tail	6.71713E-07	
t Critical one-tail	1.665151353	
P(T<=t) two-tail	1.34343E-06	
t Critical two-tail	1.99167261	

Figure 4.4 T-test for two samples assuming unequal variances

Using R for Z-Test and T-Test

Import the data file Employee into R, store the data in a data frame named emp. Enter the complete path (summarized here). We will do Z-test and T-test on two columns of data, Rate1 and Rate2.

```
emp<-data.frame(read.csv(file="C:/Users/~/Employee.csv",
header=TRUE))
```

R package BSDA provides basic statistics and data analysis tools. Install and load the library. Test the equality of variances, the assumption of z-test and t-test:

```
var.test(emp$Rate1, emp$Rate2)

F test to compare two variances
data:emp$Rate1 and emp$Rate2
F = 1.35, numdf = 39, denomdf = 39, p-value = 0.3527
alternative hypothesis: true ratio of variances is not equal to 1
95 percent confidence interval:
0.7140196 2.5524902
sample estimates:
ratio of variances
1.35001
```

The p-value of this test does not indicate significant difference of variance.

Shapiro-Wilk test of normality shows normal distribution of Rate1 (p-value=0.43), but the small p-value of this test for Rate2 is a sign of non-normal distribution of this variable.

```
>shapiro.test(emp$Rate1)

        Shapiro-Wilk normality test

data:emp$Rate1
W = 0.9725, p-value = 0.4304

>shapiro.test(emp$Rate2)

        Shapiro-Wilk normality test

data:emp$Rate2
W = 0.83777, p-value = 4.604e-05
```

We need the mean of Rate1 and standard deviation of both variables for one sample Z-test:

Use these values as arguments of z-test:

```
>z.test(emp$Rate1, emp$Rate2, mu=0, sigma.x=sd(emp$Rate1,
sigma.y=sd(emp$Rate2)

        Two-sample z-Test

data:emp$Rate1 and emp$Rate2
z = -5.2486, p-value = 1.532e-07
alternative hypothesis: true difference in means is not equal to 0
95 percent confidence interval:
-5.322014 -2.427986
sample estimates:
mean of x mean of y
13.30017.175
```

For a paired t-test we will have the following outcome. The small p-value indicates the significance of difference between two ratings.

```
>t.test(emp$Rate1, emp$Rate2, paired=TRUE)

    Paired t-test

data:emp$Rate1 and emp$Rate2
t = -4.8683, df = 39, p-value = 1.896e-05
alternative hypothesis: true difference in means is not equal to 0
95 percent confidence interval:
-5.485008 -2.264992
sample estimates:
mean of the differences
-3.875
```

Analysis of Variance

Analysis of variance (ANOVA) is a parametric test of means based on sample data where two or more samples are involved. ANOVA is based on assumptions including independent samples, normal distribution of samples, and homogeneity of variances. We will use an example of three samples to explain this method. Three different suppliers provide material for a timing chain manufacturing shop. These chains are used in a new engine, so durability and shear strength are important factors. In a pilot test, manufacturer produced small batches of chains from each material and sampled them for shear strength test. Each sample includes 30 observations. Shear strength numbers, the pressure under which the chains broke, are listed as samples A, B, and C in ANOVA worksheet of the chapter data file.

Variable used for measurement in a study is a factor, so the factor of this study is pressure (psi). A study that involves only one factor is a single-factor study. ANOVA test for one factor is a single factor ANOVA. As a test of means, ANOVA has a null hypothesis of equal means for all samples:

$$H_0: \mu_1 = \mu_2 = \mu_3$$

Alternative hypothesis states that sample means are different. At least one of the sample means is significantly different from the other samples.

$$Ha: \mu_i \neq \mu_j \text{ at least for one pair of } (i, j)$$

We can compute the variance of multiple samples in two different ways, between the samples and within the samples. The logic of ANOVA is that the variances calculated in two ways should not be significantly different if all samples belong to the same population. A significant difference between these two types of variances indicate that at least one sample mean is different from the others and does not belong to the same population. Figure 4.5 left side graph shows three samples with different means but significant overlap. These samples are assumes to belong to one hypothetical population. On the right side of this figure we can see two samples with overlap, and one sample with a very different mean. These three samples cannot belong to the same population. A vertical line shows the location of overall mean of samples. We will use this concept in computing variances.

Between the samples and within the samples variances may be close or very different. One measure that can create a single criterion of judgment is ratio of these two variances. This is F ratio:

$$F = \frac{\text{Variance between sample means}}{\text{Variance within samples}} = \frac{\text{Mean squared error between sample means}}{\text{Mean squared error within samples}}$$

There is an F critical value based on degrees of freedom of the two variances. F ratios greater than the F critical are sign of significant difference between sample means. We will discuss the F test after explaining the calculation of variances by an example. For simplicity, only the top

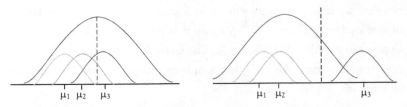

Figure 4.5 Three samples may have close means (left), or at least one of them being different (right)

five test results of each sample are included in calculations at this step. Formulas of mean squared errors between groups and within samples are as the following:

$$\text{Mean squares between groups} = \frac{\sum n(\bar{Y}_j - \bar{Y}_T)^2}{K - 1}$$

$$\text{Mean squares within samples} = \frac{\sum(Y_{ij} - \bar{Y}_j)^2}{\sum n_j - k}$$

n_j = sample j size

k = # of groups (1-k)

$\bar{Y}_j$ = group j mean

Y_{ij} = element i from group j

$\bar{Y}_T$ = Grand mean

The first step is computing the means of samples and overall mean of all observations. These values are used for calculating variances/mean squared errors.

In computing errors between samples we consider the mean of that sample as representative data of the entire sample, and calculate its deviation from the overall mean. Formulas in range H2:J2 in Figure 4.6 demonstrate this. Each observation is represented by the same value in computing mean squared errors, so these formulas are repeated for all observations in columns H, I, and J. We need to square these deviations and add them up for total sum of squared errors. Excel SUMPRODUCT function does all these calculations in one step. Formula in cell H8 in Figure 4.6 demonstrates SUMPRODUCT function and its arguments. Both arguments are the data range H2:J6.

	A	B	C	D	E	F	G	H	I	J
1	A	B	C				Between A		B	C
2	2244	2001	1923					=B$7-$B$8	=C$7-$B$8	=D$7-$B$8
3	1897	2047	1847					=B$7-$B$8	=C$7-$B$8	=D$7-$B$8
4	1897	1895	1873					=B$7-$B$8	=C$7-$B$8	=D$7-$B$8
5	1868	1971	2095					=B$7-$B$8	=C$7-$B$8	=D$7-$B$8
6	2132	1873	2258					=B$7-$B$8	=C$7-$B$8	=D$7-$B$8
7	Sample Mean	=AVERAGE(B2:B6)	=AVERAGE(C2:C6)	=AVERAGE(D2:D6)						
8	Grand Average	=AVERAGE(B2:D6)					SS$_{between}$	=SUMPRODUCT(H2:J6,H2:J6)		
9							df=	=3-1		
10							MS$_{between}$	=H8/H9		

Figure 4.6 Three sample test of means. Mean squared errors between groups

Degree of freedom for sum of squares deviation is 2. We have three samples and one statistic, the mean. Degree of freedom is 3–1=2. Mean squared error between the samples is calculated in cell H10 by dividing sum of squared errors by degree of freedom.

Calculating mean squared errors between samples follows a similar process by finding deviations of each observation from mean of the group. Range M2:O6 in Figure 4.7 shows computing deviations from sample means. We then use Excel SUMPRODUCT function in cell M8 to compute sum of squared deviations. We have 15 observations in these three samples and three sample means that should stay constant, so degree of freedom for sum of squared errors within samples is 12. Mean squares error is the ratio of sum of squared errors over degree of freedom. This value is in cell M10. F ratio is calculated in cell Q10 by dividing mean squared errors between samples by mean squared errors within samples. This F value is 0.16846.

Using standard F tables, we can find the F critical value. Using F tables (Figure 4.8) requires using degrees of freedom for numerator and denominator of the F ration. These degrees of freedom are 2 and 12 respectively, so we can find the critical value for given alpha level. A=0.05 has a critical F value of 3.89. Since our computed F ratio is 0.16846, a number less than the critical value, we fail to reject the null hypothesis. Sample means are considered equal. We used a small number of observations for demonstrating ANOVA process. All observations will be used in ANOVA test using Excel data analysis Toolpak.

Using Excel data analysis Toolpak for single factor ANOVA.

Data file ANOVA worksheet contains three samples, each with 30 observations. Single factor ANOVA is the first tool in data analysis

	K	L	M	N	O	P	Q
1		Within	A	B	C		
2			=B2-B$7	=C2-C$7	=D2-D$7		
3			=B3-B$7	=C3-C$7	=D3-D$7		
4			=B4-B$7	=C4-C$7	=D4-D$7		
5			=B5-B$7	=C5-C$7	=D5-D$7		
6			=B6-B$7	=C6-C$7	=D6-D$7		
7							
8		SS$_{within}$	=SUMPRODUCT(M2:O6,M2:O6)				
9		df=	=3*(5-1)				
10		MS$_{within}$	=M8/M9			F =	=H10/M10

Figure 4.7 Three sample test of means. Mean squared errors within samples, and F ratio

		p	1	2	3	4	5	6
							Degrees of freedom in the numerator	
	11	.100	3.23	2.86	2.66	2.54	2.45	2.39
		.050	4.84	3.98	3.59	3.36	3.20	3.09
		.025	6.72	5.26	4.63	4.28	4.04	3.88
		.010	9.65	7.21	6.22	5.67	5.32	5.07
		.001	19.69	13.81	11.56	10.35	9.58	9.05
	12	.100	3.18	2.81	2.61	2.48	2.39	2.33
		.050	4.75	3.89	3.49	3.26	3.11	3.00
		.025	6.55	5.10	4.47	4.12	3.89	3.73
		.010	9.33	6.93	5.95	5.41	5.06	4.82
		.001	18.64	12.97	10.80	9.63	8.89	8.38
	13	.100	3.14	2.76	2.56	2.43	2.35	2.28
		.050	4.67	3.81	3.41	3.18	3.03	2.92
		.025	6.41	4.97	4.35	4.00	3.77	3.60
		.010	9.07	6.70	5.74	5.21	4.86	4.62
		.001	17.82	12.31	10.21	9.07	8.35	7.86
		.100	3.10	2.73	2.52	2.39	2.31	2.24

Degrees of freedom in the denominator (vertical axis label)

Figure 4.8 F table

Toolpak. The dialog box is simple. We need to organize samples in adjacent columns or rows and pass them to the dialog box as one range. Alpha level of 0.05 is used in this example. After clicking OK we will see the analysis output. In ANOVA table the calculated F ratio for 90 observations is 3.67 and F critical is 3.10. Since the computed F ratio is larger than critical F, we reject the null hypothesis and conclude that mean shear strengths of three samples are significantly different. The P-value is computed as 0.029 that is less than 0.05, the significance level of this test (Figure 4.9).

At this point, we look at the basic assumptions of ANOVA, homogeneity of variances and normal distribution of samples.

A skewed distribution is a sign of deviation from normality. Excel data analysis Toolpak can generate descriptive statistics for each data set including skewness, mean, median, maximum, and minimum. Skewness within the range of −1.96 and +1.96 and kurtosis within the range of −2 to +2, are acceptable for a normal distribution.

Cumulative distribution function (CDF) demonstrates deviations from normal distribution. Figure 4.10 shows the formulas and graph. First step is to sort observations from smallest to largest. Then compute a column of numbers where each observation of data has equal share of the percentage of observations. Selecting columns A, B, and C and creating a line graph will project values in columns B and C as lines,

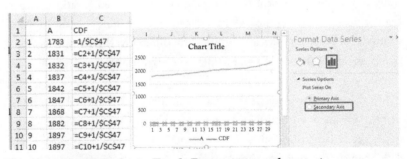

Anova: Single Factor

SUMMARY

Groups	Count	Sum	Average	Variance
A	30	59902	1996.733	18057.79
B	30	58435	1947.833	10804.9
C	30	61161	2038.7	21826.01

ANOVA

Source of Variation	SS	df	MS	F	P-value	F crit
Between Groups	124091.6	2	62045.81	3.672168	0.029441	3.101296
Within Groups	1469972	87	16896.23			
Total	1594064	89				

Figure 4.9 Single factor ANOVA dialog box and output

	A	B	C
1		A	CDF
2	1	1783	=1/$C$47
3	2	1831	=C2+1/$C$47
4	3	1832	=C3+1/$C$47
5	4	1837	=C4+1/$C$47
6	5	1842	=C5+1/$C$47
7	6	1847	=C6+1/$C$47
8	7	1868	=C7+1/$C$47
9	8	1882	=C8+1/$C$47
10	9	1897	=C9+1/$C$47
11	10	1897	=C10+1/$C$47

Figure 4.10 CDF plot in Excel. Projecting one data series on secondary axis

sharing the same vertical axis. CDF column creates a gradually increasing value, graphically a straight line, as a base of comparison for proportions of real data at each percentile. Calculations are in column C. Count of sample observations is in cell C47, which is referenced in formulas. Each cell adds the value of the cell on top of it, plus 1/30 (30 is the count of observations).

Right-click the CDF line which is almost entirely on horizontal axis due to its small values. From screen menu select "Format Data Series" to open this pane. Select "Series Options" icon and then select "Secondary Axis." This will create a second vertical axis to the right scaled for the range of CDF data, and projects CDF line on this axis.

After projecting CDF column values on secondary axis, adjust the minimum and maximum values of primary and secondary axis to values near the range of actual data. For primary axis these limits are 1,700 and 2,300, and for secondary axis 0 and 1. Figure 4.11 shows Format Axis tool for primary axis adjustment. Double-click primary axis (left vertical axis of the chart) to open Format Axis box. Select Axis Options icon, expand Axis Options and enter values for minimum and maximum bounds. These values should contain all observations, but truncate the additional space on graph since graphs usually start from point zero. Repeat the same process for the secondary axis to limit values between 0 and 1. Points of a perfectly normal distribution will be all along the CDF line. We can observe deviations from normal, but this much of deviation does not show serious skewness. We can observe from the graph that the mean of 1996.7 (on the primary axis) is around 50th percentile of the data (on the secondary axis). In a normal distribution, about 95 percent of the data should be within +/-2 standard deviations from the mean.

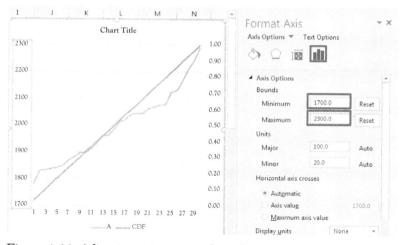

Figure 4.11 Adjusting primary axis bounds

Calculated standard deviation of sample A is 134.38.+/–2 standard deviations from the mean is the range of 1728 to 2265. As the graph shows this range includes almost the entire data set. These observations indicate that the data set is acceptable as normal distribution.

Homogeneity of Variance

Another assumption of ANOVA is homogeneity of variance. Based on this assumption, variances of all samples used in ANOVA should not be significantly different. There are multiple tests for homogeneity of variances, we will explain Levene test here. The null hypothesis of all tests of unequal variances is equality of variances:

$$H_0: \sigma_1^2 = \sigma_2^2 = ... = \sigma_k^2$$

Alternative hypothesis states that at least one of the variances is significantly different from others.

$$H_a: \sigma_i^2 \neq \sigma_j^2 \text{ for some pair of } (i,j)$$

Levene test calculates W statistic that is F distributed. The P-value of F test less than the alpha level (usually 0.05) rejects the null hypothesis of equal variances. The formula of W is:

$$w = \frac{(N-K)}{K-1} \frac{\sum_{i=1}^{k} N_i (\bar{Z}_{i.} - \bar{Z}_{..})^2}{\sum_{i=1}^{k} \sum_{j=1}^{N_i} (\bar{Z}_{ij} - \bar{Z}_{i.})^2}$$

N = total number of observations in all samples (groups)
K = Number of samples (groups)
N_i = Sample i size
$Z_{i.}$ = mean of the Z_{ij} for group i
Z_{ij} = absolute deviation of each observation from sample mean
$Z_{..}$ = mean of all absolute deviations from sample means

Leven's formula for unequal variance test is quite similar to the formula of F ratio for ANOVA, with a difference that observations are replaced by absolute value of deviations from the mean. We do ANOVA

Anova: Single Factor

SUMMARY

Groups	Count	Sum	Average	Variance
A-deviations	30	3360	112	5081.237
B-deviations	30	2561	85.36667	3266.143
C-deviations	30	3601.6	120.0533	6916.214

ANOVA

Source of Variation	SS	df	MS	F	P-value	F crit
Between Groups	19773.55	2	9886.777	1.943208	0.149411	3.101296
Within Groups	442644.2	87	5087.865			
Total	462417.8	89				

Figure 4.12 ANOVA for absolute deviations from mean of samples. Means are in row 33

test for deviations and the P-value of the F test will determine if the assumption of homogeneity of variances is met. Figure 4.12 shows formulas for calculating deviations from the sample means, using data file Levene worksheet. Use Single factor ANOVA from data analysis Toolpak and enter input range of E1:G31. Analysis output P-value for F test is 0.1494, which is larger than alpha level of 0.05 and fails to reject the null hypothesis of equal variances. The data meets homogeneity of variance assumption. Since sample data distributions are normal as well, ANOVA is a valid test of means.

ANOVA in R

Import Chain data file into R and store values in a data frame, chain.

```
chain<-data.frame(read.csv(file="C://users/s-mnabavi1/Downloads/
Chain.csv"))
```

Gather observations in one column "gather" function needs dplyr and tidyr packages. Install these packages, load the libraries. Name the new factor column "group" and observation column "data."

```
>library(tidyr)
>library(deplyr)
>chain_g<- gather(group, data, A, B, C, data=chain)
```

Levene test of unequal variances requires lawstat package. Install this package if not installed yet, and load the library:

```
>library(lawstat)

>leveneTest(chain_g$data, chain_g$group, data=chain_g)
Levene'sTest for Homogeneity of Variance (center = median: chain_g)
Df F value Pr(>F)
group21.9135 0.1537
87
```

Levene test results show that variances are not significantly different. If Shapio-Wilk test results show normality of the groups as well, we will do ANOVA test.

```
>res<- aov(data~ group, data=chain_g)
>summary(res)
DfSum Sq Mean Sq F value Pr(>F)
group2124092620463.672 0.0294 *
Residuals87 146997216896
---
Signif.codes:0 '***' 0.001 '**' 0.01 '*' 0.05 '.' 0.1 ' ' 1
```

P-value of 0.0294 indicates significance of differences among mean strengths of materials.

Nonparametric Tests of Means

Z-test, t-test, and ANOVA are based on the assumption of normal distribution. ANOVA has additional assumption for homogeneity of variances. If the data is not parametric, or assumptions of each test are not met, parametric tests are not valid. We will use nonparametric tests instead. Here we explain two nonparametric tests. Mann-Whitney and signed rank Wilcoxon test are nonparametric test of means for two groups. Mann-Whitney is a test of two treatments or two independent samples. Wilcoxon is a test of paired samples, where each subject is measured twice and the outcome of each measurement is a member of one sample. Kruskal-Wallis is a nonparametric test of means for more than two groups.

Mann-Whitney and Wilcoxon test: When the two samples being compared are not normally distributed, particularly for small samples, Wilcoxon signed-rank test of means is an alternative for paired samples and Mann-Whitney test for independent samples. Both tests have similar hypotheses, but Mann-Whitney hypothesis is stated in terms of rank and Wilcoxon in terms of signed rank. Mann-Whitney states that average rank of one treatment is significantly different than the average rank of the other.

Null hypothesis for Mann-Whitney test: ranks of observations for one treatment do not tend to be systematically higher or lower than the ranks of another treatment. Two treatments do not make a difference.

Alternative hypothesis for Mann-Whitney test: ranks of observations for one treatment are systematically higher or lower than another treatment. Two treatments make a difference.

We use a subset of the customer rating data for this example to determine if training program made a significant different in customer satisfaction. 10 customer ratings were selected from each group, before and after training.

The test process requires ranking all scores from both samples. Then each observation of one sample, has lower rank than how many observations from the other sample. We can demonstrate this process as Excel worksheet formulas in Figure 4.13. Rate observations are in column B and Group labels are in column A. Data is sorted ascendingly based on values in column B, than Rank added as a sequence of incrementing number in column C. The U value in column D is obtained by an IF statement which check for group in column 1, and counts the members of the other group below it (with higher rank) through the end of the data using a conditional count function. Note the referencing of values in column A that allows us for creating this formula once in row 2 and copying it down for all values.

Sum of U values for group 1 and 2 are calculated in cells G3 and G4, using a conditional summation function. U1=83 and U2=17. Total U values is 100 which is equal to $n_1 n_2$ (10×10). A large difference between U_1 and U_2 is a sign of significantly different ranks between the two groups. The test statistic U is the smaller of the two U values, Min(83, 17)=17 (Figure 4.13).

Mann-Whitney tables (Figure 4.14) provide critical values of U for different alpha levels. We reject the null hypothesis of no difference for U values less than the critical U. Both groups in our test have 10 observations and Nondirectional alpha level is 0.05, so the critical U value is 23. Calculated U value of the data is 17, Less than the critical value. Therefore

	A	B	C	D	E	F	G
1	Group	Rate	Rank	Points (U)			
2	Rate1	6	1	=IF(A2="Rate1", COUNTIF(A3:$A$21, "Rate2"), COUNTIF(A3:$A$21, "Rate1"))			
3	Rate1	8	2	=IF(A3="Rate1", COUNTIF(A4:$A$21, "Rate2"), COUNTIF(A4:$A$21, "Rate1"))		U₁	=SUMIF($A$2:$A$81,"Rate1",$D$2:$D$81)
4	Rate2	13	3	=IF(A5="Rate1", COUNTIF(A5:$A$21, "Rate2"), COUNTIF(A5:$A$21, "Rate1"))		U₂	=SUMIF($A$2:$A$81,"Rate2",$D$2:$D$81)
5	Rate1	14	4	=IF(A5="Rate1", COUNTIF(A6:$A$21, "Rate2"), COUNTIF(A6:$A$21, "Rate1"))		U₁+U₂	=G4+G3
6	Rate1	14	5	=IF(A6="Rate1", COUNTIF(A7:$A$21, "Rate2"), COUNTIF(A7:$A$21, "Rate1"))			
7	Rate1	15	6	=IF(A7="Rate1", COUNTIF(A8:$A$21, "Rate2"), COUNTIF(A8:$A$21, "Rate1"))			
8	Rate1	15	7	=IF(A8="Rate1". COUNTIF(A9:$A$21. "Rate2"). COUNTIF(A9:$A$21. "Rate1"))			

Figure 4.13 *Assigning Mann-Whitney U values to all observations*

					Nondirectional α=.05 (Directional α=.025)									
									n_2					
n_1	1	2	3	4	5	6	7	8	9	10	11	12	13	14	15
1	-	-	-	-	-	-	-	-	-		-	-	-	-	-
2	-	-	-	-	-	-	-	0	0	0	0	1	1	1	1
3	-	-	-	-	0	1	1	2	2	3	3	4	4	5	5
4	-	-	-	0	1	2	3	4	4	5	6	7	8	9	10
5	-	-	0	1	2	3	5	6	7	8	9	11	12	13	14
6	-	-	1	2	3	5	6	8	10	11	13	14	16	17	19
7	-	-	1	3	5	6	8	10	12	14	16	18	20	22	24
8	-	0	2	4	6	8	10	13	15	17	19	22	24	26	29
9	-	0	2	4	7	10	12	15	17	21	23	26	28	31	34
10	-	0	3	5	8	11	14	17	20	23	26	29	33	36	39
11	-	0	3	6	9	13	16	19	23	26	30	33	37	40	44

Figure 4.14 *Mann-Whitney U table*

we reject the null hypothesis and conclude that the two group means are significantly different.

Wilcoxon signed rank test: this test is used for evaluating difference between treatments on paired samples. For each pair, the difference of two treatments has a positive or negative sign. For example if one of the scores is before treatment and one after the treatment, higher than the score before, subtracting the initial score from after treatment will be a positive number. A lower score after treatment will generate a negative number since we are subtracting a larger number from a smaller one. Next step is ranking these differences based on their absolute value, in ascending order. Rank 1 is the smallest absolute value and highest rank is the largest absolute value of differences. We use customer ranking data from Wilcoxon worksheet of the data file for this test (Figure 4.15). To compute the ranks in Excel, add a column for absolute value of differences and use it as a reference in RANK.AVG( ) function. This function assigns average ranks for tied values. For example, absolute value of six difference scores is "1" and all need to receive the lowest rank. They all receive the average rank, $(1+2+3+4+5+6)/6=3.5$.

Null hypothesis of Wilcoxon test states that signs of score differences are not systematically positive or negative. Treatment does not make a difference. If this is true, positive and negative differences must be evenly mixed.

Alternative hypothesis of Wilcoxon test states that difference score signs are systematically positive or negative. There is a difference due to treatment.

After ranking differences, we will add up all ranks for positive signs together, as well as ranks for negative signs. The smaller sum of ranks is the Wilcoxon T statistic. We use Excel conditional summation SUMIF( ) function for this calculation as demonstrated in Figure 4.16, in cells I2

Figure 4.15 Signed difference score and ranks for paired samples, formula and results

	A	B	C	D	E	F	G	H	I
1	Employee	Rate1	Rate2	Difference	ABS Dif	Rank			
2	1	9	13	=C2-B2	=ABS(D2)	=RANK.AVG(E2,$E$2:$E$41,1)		Negative sign ranks	=SUMIF($D$2:$D$41,"<0",$F$2:$F$41)
3	2	13	15	=C3-B3	=ABS(D3)	=RANK.AVG(E3,$E$2:$E$41,1)		Positive sign ranks	=SUMIF($D$2:$D$41,">0",$F$2:$F$41)
4	3	11	20	=C4-B4	=ABS(D4)	=RANK.AVG(E4,$E$2:$E$41,1)			
5	4	8	20	=C5-B5	=ABS(D5)	=RANK.AVG(E5,$E$2:$E$41,1)			
6	5	16	20	=C6-B6	=ABS(D6)	=RANK.AVG(E6,$E$2:$E$41,1)			
7	6	11	17	=C7-B7	=ABS(D7)	=RANK.AVG(E7,$E$2:$E$41,1)			
8	7	15	18	=C8-B8	=ABS(D8)	=RANK.AVG(E8,$E$2:$E$41,1)			

Figure 4.16 Positive and negative ranks summation

$\alpha1=$	5%	2.5%	1%	0.5%		$\alpha1=$	5%	2.5%	1%	0.5%
n $\alpha2=$	10%	5%	2%	1%	n $\alpha2=$	10%	5%	2%	1%
1	—	—	—	—	26	110	98	84	75
2	—	—	—	—	27	119	107	92	83
3	—	—	—	—	28	130	116	101	91
13	21	17	12	9	38	256	235	211	194
14	25	21	15	12	39	271	249	224	207
15	30	25	19	15	40	286	264	238	220

Figure 4.17 Wilcoxon table of critical values

and I3. Positive signed ranks in our example added up to 697.5 and negative signed ranks to 122.5, so the Wilcoxon T is the minimum of the two. T = 122.5.

This is a one-tail test since we expect the scores to be higher after training. In Wilcoxon table of critical values (Figure 4.17), we find the critical value of 286 for a one-tail test, sample size 40, and alpha level of 5 percent. Our sample T is 122.5, smaller than the critical value. Therefore, we reject the null hypothesis of signs being evenly mixed, and conclude that customer ratings significantly increased after training.

Wilcoxon Test in R

Use "emp" data frame for Wilcoxon test.

```
>wilcox.test(emp$Rate1, emp$Rate2, paired=TRUE)

    Wilcoxon signed rank test with continuity correction

data:emp$Rate1 and emp$Rate2
V = 110.5, p-value = 5.705e-05
alternative hypothesis: true location shift is not equal to 0
```

	A	B	C	D	E	F	G
1	A	B	C		A	B	C
2	2244	2001	1923		=RANK.AVG(A2,$A$2:$C$31,1)	=RANK.AVG(B2,$A$2:$C$31,1)	=RANK.AVG(C2,$A$2:$C$31,1)
3	1897	2047	1847		=RANK.AVG(A3,$A$2:$C$31,1)	=RANK.AVG(B3,$A$2:$C$31,1)	=RANK.AVG(C3,$A$2:$C$31,1)
4	1897	1895	1873		=RANK.AVG(A4,$A$2:$C$31,1)	=RANK.AVG(B4,$A$2:$C$31,1)	=RANK.AVG(C4,$A$2:$C$31,1)
5	1868	1971	2095		=RANK.AVG(A5,$A$2:$C$31,1)	=RANK.AVG(B5,$A$2:$C$31,1)	=RANK.AVG(C5,$A$2:$C$31,1)
6	2132	1873	2258		=RANK.AVG(A6,$A$2:$C$31,1)	=RANK.AVG(B6,$A$2:$C$31,1)	=RANK.AVG(C6,$A$2:$C$31,1)
7	1985	1860	1794		=RANK.AVG(A7,$A$2:$C$31,1)	=RANK.AVG(B7,$A$2:$C$31,1)	=RANK.AVG(C7,$A$2:$C$31,1)
8	1842	2106	1903		=RANK.AVG(A8,$A$2:$C$31,1)	=RANK.AVG(B8,$A$2:$C$31,1)	=RANK.AVG(C8,$A$2:$C$31,1)

Figure 4.18 Rank orders for three samples

Kruskal-Wallis test: This nonparametric test is used for comparing means of more than two groups. This is an alternative test for single-factor ANOVA that does not require numerical factors as long as we are able to rank sample observations, similar to Mann-Whitney test but without the limitation of only two groups. Kruskal-Wallis test compares three or more independent samples or results of different treatments. Data used for Kruskal-Wallis test must be ordinal. Original data may be ordinal, or the ranks of all observations used as ordinal data for this test. We will use the three samples of timing chain shear strength for this example. Figure 4.18 shows formulas for ranking these three samples. Each number is compared to the entire set of all three samples. Average ranking used for ties and ranks are in ascending order.

Each group will have a total rank score or T value. This value is used for comparing groups.

Null hypothesis of Kruskal-Wallis test states that ranks do not tend to be systematically higher or lower than other groups or treatments. There are no differences between groups.

Alternative hypothesis of this test states that at least one treatment is different than the others, so its ranks are systematically higher or lower than the other groups.

Kruskal-Wallis test has a distribution that approximates by χ^2 (Chi-Square). This test is used for goodness of fit and proportions of a multinomial population. For example if there is no difference among the shear strengths of chains from three different materials and sample sizes are equal, observed frequency of each material is 1/3. Expected frequency of failures under pressure below 2,000 psi also must be 1/3 for each group. Any significant deviation from that proportion shows a difference between materials. χ^2 test formula is:

$$\chi^2 = \Sigma \left[\frac{(\text{Observed frequency} - \text{expected frequency})^2}{\text{Expected frequency}} \right] \quad \text{or:}$$

$$\chi^2 = \Sigma_{i=1}^{k} \frac{(f_i - e_i)^2}{e_i}$$

In which:

f_i = observed frequency of category i

e_i = expected frequency of category i

K = number of categories

We use Kruskal-Wallis H statistic in χ^2 standard tables, given the degree of freedom for the data.

H values greater than critical value reject the null hypothesis of no difference among groups, and supports the hypothesis that states there are significant deviations from expected observations.

H statistic for Kruskal-Wallis is computed by the following formula:

$$H = \frac{12}{N(N+1)} \sum_{j=1}^{g} \frac{T_j^2}{n_j} - 3(N+1)$$

N = Total observations in all samples

n_j = Sample size of group j

g = number of groups

T_j = Total ranks in group j

In case of a rank order test the logic of χ^2 is that with no difference among the groups, ranks must be distributed through the data, proportional to sample sizes. A significant deviation from proportions will cause a concentration of ranks in one direction. Degree of freedom is defined by number of groups minus one, so for three groups degree of freedom is 3–1=2. Figure 4.19 shows Excel formulas for calculating H statistic of the test. Formulas in row 2 calculate total ranks for each sample. Formula in cell J3 references these values to calculate H=6.24.

H	I	J	K	L
		A	B	C
	Total (T)	=SUM(E2:E31)	=SUM(F2:F31)	=SUM(G2:G31)
	H=	=12/(90*(90+1))*(J2^2/30+K2^2/30+L2^2/30)-3*(90+1)		

df	$\chi^2_{.995}$	$\chi^2_{.990}$	$\chi^2_{.975}$	$\chi^2_{.950}$	$\chi^2_{.900}$	$\chi^2_{.100}$	$\chi^2_{.050}$	$\chi^2_{.025}$	$\chi^2_{.010}$	$\chi^2_{.005}$
1	0.000	0.000	0.001	0.004	0.016	2.706	3.841	5.024	6.635	7.879
2	0.010	0.020	0.051	0.103	0.211	4.605	5.991	7.378	9.210	10.597
3	0.072	0.115	0.216	0.352	0.584	6.251	7.815	9.348	11.345	12.838
4	0.207	0.297	0.484	0.711	1.064	7.779	9.488	11.143	13.277	14.860
5	0.412	0.554	0.831	1.145	1.610	9.236	11.070	12.833	15.086	16.750

Figure 4.19 χ^2 Distribution table

IB

Using χ^2 distribution table and degree of freedom 2, the computed critical value of 6.24 is greater than 5.991, but not from the next level critical value, 7.378. At alpha level 0.05 this result indicates significant difference among the samples. At least one of the samples is significantly different from the others (Figure 4.19).

R Solution for Kruskal-Wallis Test

Use chain_g data frame to do nonparametric test of means, Kruskal-Wallis. A very small p-value demonstrates the significance of differences among means of observations for groups A, B, and C.

```
kruskal.test(data, group, data=chain_g)

        Kruskal-Wallis rank sum test

data:data
Kruskal-Wallis chi-squared = 87.547, df = 4, p-value < 2.2e-16
```

CHAPTER 5

Linear Regression

Forecasting time series is an important tool in quantitative business analysis. This chapter is primarily about linear regression. We begin with simple regression, meaning one independent variable. This is very often useful in time series analysis, with Time as the independent variable. Our focus is on linear regression, but we will compare with moving average because it is a simple approach that often does better than linear regression if seasonality or cyclical components are present in the data. Regression is a basic statistical tool. In data mining, it is one of the basic tools for analysis, used in classification applications through logistic regression and discriminant analysis, as well as prediction of continuous data through ordinary least squares (OLS) and other forms. As such, regression is often taught in one (or more) three-hour courses. We cannot hope to cover all of the basics of regression. However, we here present ways in which regression is used within the context of data mining.

Time Series Forecasting

The data set we will use for demonstration in this chapter is the percent change in real gross domestic product of the United States, measured in billions of dollars adjusted to 2009 to account for inflation. The data is quarterly, which the Federal Reserve has seasonally adjusted. The source is www.bea.gov/national/pdf/nipaguid.pdf, which at the time we downloaded provided quarterly data from 1st quarter 1947 through 1st quarter 2018 (observation 284).

Moving Average Models

The idea behind moving average models is quite simply to take the n last observations and divide by n to obtain a forecast. This can and has been

Table 5.1 Moving average forecasts—U.S. GDP

Quarter	Time	GDP		2pd	3pd	4pd
I 2017	293	16903.24				
II 2017	294	17031.09				
III 2017	295	17163.89				
IV 2017	296	17286.5				
I 2018	297	17371.85				
II 2018	298			17329.18	17274.08	17213.33

modified to weight various components, but our purpose is to simply demonstrate how it works. Table 5.1 shows the last five quarterly observations, which is then used to generate two-period, three-period, and four-period forecasts.

In Table 5.1, the two period moving average is simply the average of the prior two observations, or 17286.5 and 17371.85. Three and four period moving averages extend these one additional period back. These outcomes have the feature that for relatively volatile time series, the closer to the present you are, the more accurate the forecast. Moving average has the advantage of being quick and easy. As a forecast, it only extends one period into the future, which is a limitation. If there was a seasonal cycle, the 12-period moving average might be a very good forecast. But the GDP data set provided is already seasonally adjusted.

There are lots of error metrics for time series forecasts. We will use mean squared error (MSE) (to compare with regression output from Excel). This goes back to the beginning of the time series, makes two, three, and four period moving averages, squares the difference between observed and forecasted over all past observations, and averages these squared differences. For the two-period moving average this MSE was 13,740, for the three-period moving average 22,553, and for the four-period moving average 33,288.

Regression Models

Regression is used on a variety of data types. If data is time series, output from regression models is often used for forecasting. Regression can be used to build predictive models for other types of data. Regression can be applied in a number of different forms. The class of regression models is a major class of tools available to support the Modeling phase of the data mining process.

Probably the most widely used data mining algorithms are data fitting, in the sense of regression. Regression is a fundamental tool for statistical analysis to characterize relationships between a dependent variable and one or more independent variables. Regression models can be used for many purposes, to include explanation and prediction. Linear and logistic regression models are both primary tools in most general purpose data mining software. Nonlinear data can sometimes be transformed into useful linear data and analyzed with linear regression. Some special forms of nonlinear regression also exist.

OLS regression is a model of the form:

$$Y = \beta_0 + \beta_1 X_1 + \beta_2 X_2 + \dots + \beta_n X_n + \varepsilon$$

where Y is the dependent variable (the one being forecast),
X_n are the n independent (explanatory) variables,
β_0 is the intercept term,
β_n are the n coefficients for the independent variables,
ε is the error term.

OLS regression is the straight line (with intercept and slope coefficients β_n) which minimizes the sum of squared error (SSE) terms ε_i over all i observations. The idea is that you look at past data to determine the β coefficients which worked best. The model gives you the most likely future value of the dependent variable given knowledge of the X_n for future observations. This approach assumes a linear relationship, and error terms that are normally distributed around zero without patterns. While these assumptions are often unrealistic, regression is highly attractive because of the existence of widely available computer packages as well as highly developed statistical theory. Statistical packages provide the probability that estimated parameters differ from zero.

Excel offers a variety of useful business analytic tools through the Data Analysis Toolpak add-in. Many students have used this suite of analytic tools before, but for those who have not, getting started has often proved challenging. We thus append a walk-through of adding this feature to your Excel software.

We can apply regression to the problem of extending a trend line. We will use the quarterly GDP data to demonstrate. The dependent variable (Y) is the quarterly GDP over the period I 1947 through I 2018. The independent variable (X) is time, an index of weeks beginning with one and ending at 285, the last available observation. Figure 5.1 displays this data.

This data is a little erratic, and notably nonlinear. OLS regression fits this data with the straight line that minimizes the SSE terms. Given the data's nonlinearity, we don't expect a very good fit, but the OLS model does show average trend. Here the model is:

$$Y = \beta_0 + \beta_1 X + \varepsilon$$

where Y is Requests and X is the quarter with 1 being I 1947:

The regression output from Excel for our data is shown in Table 5.2.

This output provides a great deal of information. We will discuss regression statistics, which measure the fit of the model to the data, in the following. ANOVA information is an overall test of the model itself.

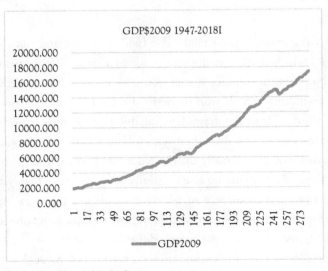

Figure 5.1 Graph of GDP data

Table 5.2 Regression output for GDP time series

SUMMARY OUTPUT						
Regression Statistics						
Multiple R	0.982					
R Square	0.965					
Adj R Square	0.965					
Standard Error	881.603					
Observations	285					
ANOVA						
	Df	*SS*	*MS*	*F*	*Significance F*	
Regression	1	6066752726	6066752726	7805.673	4.431E– 208	
Residual	283	219954255.4	777223.517			
Total	284	6286706981				
	Coefficients	*Standard Error*	*t Stat*	*P-value*	*Lower 95%*	*Upper 95%*
Intercept	15.132	104.719	0.144	0.885	–190.995	221.258
Time	56.080	0.635	88.350	4.4308E-208	54.830	57.329

The value for *Significance F* gives the probability that the model has no information about the dependent variable. Here, 4.431E-208 is practically zero (move the decimal place 28 digits to the left, resulting in a lot of zeros). MS for the Residual is the MSE, which can be compared to the moving average forecasts mentioned previously. Here the value of 777223.5 is worse than any of the three moving average forecasts we calculated. Finally, at the bottom of the report, is what we were after, the regression model.

$$GDP = 15.132 + 56.080 \times Time$$

Where Time = 1st quarter 1947, and Time = 286 Quarter II 2–18. This enables us to predict GDP in billions of dollars into the future. It is tempting to extrapolate this model far into the future, which violates the assumptions of regression model. But extrapolation is the model's purpose in prediction. The analyst needs to realize that the model error is

Table 5.3 Time series forecasts of GDP

Quarter	GDP$2009	Time	Regression	2pdMA	3pdMA	4pdMA
2018-04-01	17371.854	286	16054	17329	17274	17213
2018-07-01		287	16110	NA	NA	NA
2018-10-01		288	16166	NA	NA	NA
2019-01-01		289	16222	NA	NA	NA

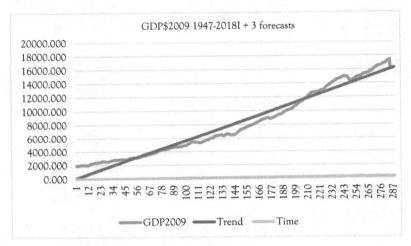

Figure 5.2 Graph of time series model

expected to grow the farther the model is projected beyond the data set upon which it was built. To forecast, multiply the time index by 56.080 and add 15.132. The forecasts for quarters 286 through 289 are given in Table 5.3.

The graphical picture of this model is given in Figure 5.2.

Clearly this OLS forecast is way off. It predicts GDP in 2018I to be 16,054, when the actual is 17,372. Moving average is much closer, but moving average is very close-sighted, and can't be extended into the future like regression models can.

Time Series Error Metrics

The classical tests of regression models are based on the assumption that errors are normally distributed around the mean, with no patterns. The basis of regression accuracy are the residuals, or difference between prediction and observed values. Residuals are then extended to a general measure of regression fit, R-squared.

SSE: The accuracy of any predictive or forecasting model can be assessed by calculating the SSE. In the regression we just completed, SSE is 219,954,255, an enormous number meaning very little by itself (it is a function not only of error, but of the number of observations). Each observation's residual (error) is the difference between actual and predicted. The sign doesn't matter, because the next step is to square each of these errors. The more accurate the model is, the lower its SSE. An SSE doesn't mean much by itself. But it is a very good way of comparing alternative models, if there are equal opportunities for each model to have error.

R^2: SSE can be used to generate more information for a particular model. The statistic R^2 is the ratio of variance explained by the model over total variance in the data. Total squared values (6,286,706,981 in our example) is explained squared dependent variable values (6,066,752,726 in our example) plus SSE (219,954,255 in our example). To obtain R^2, square the deviation of predicted or forecast values from the mean of the dependent variable values, add them up (yielding MSR), and divide MSR by (MSR + SSE). This gives the ratio of change in the dependent variable explained by the model (6,066,752,726/6,286,706,981 = 0.9650 in our example). R^2 can range from a minimum of 0 (the model tells you absolutely nothing about the dependent variable) to 1.0 (the model is perfect).

$$R^2 = \frac{SST - SSE}{SST}$$

where SST is the sum of squared deviations of the dependent variable from its own mean,

SSE is the sum of squared error (difference between actual dependent variable values and predicted or forecast values).

There are basic error metrics for general time series forecasts. The regression models from Excel report SSE as we have just seen. Another way to describe SSE is to take error for each observation, square these, and sum over the entire data set. Calculating the mean of SSE provides

MSE. An alternative error metric often used is mean absolute deviation (MAD), which is the same thing except that instead of squaring errors, absolute values are taken. MAD is considered more robust than MSE, in that a very large error will affect MSE much more than MAD. But both provide useful means of comparing the relative accuracy of time series, given that they compare models over exactly the same data. A more general error metric is mean absolute percentage error. Here the error for each observation is calculated as a percentage of the actual observation, and averaging over the entire time series.

Seasonality

Seasonality is a basic concept—cyclical data often has a tendency to be higher or lower than average in a given time period. For monthly data, we can identify each month's average relative to the overall year. Here we have quarterly data, which is deseasonalized, so we expect no seasonality. But we can demonstrate how seasonality is calculated. We calculate the average by quarter from our data set for quarters I through IV over the data set (1947–1st quarter 2018). Table 5.4 shows these averages.

The calculation is trivial—using the Average function in Excel for data by quarter and the overall average for entire series. Note that there is a bit of bias because of trend, which we will consider in time series regression. Nonetheless, this data shows no seasonality, indicating that the bureau of commerce does a good job of deseasonalizing GDP.

We can include seasonality into the regression against Time by using dummy variables for each quarter (0 if that observation is not the quarter in question—one if it is). This approach requires skipping one time

Table 5.4 Seasonality indexes by month—Brent crude oil

Quarter	Average	Season Index
I	8156.630	1.001
II	8089.151	0.993
III	8145.194	1.000
IV	8195.525	1.006
Year	8146.660	

period's dummy variable or else the model would be overspecified, and OLS wouldn't work. We'll skip quarter IV. An extract of this data is shown in Table 5.5.

Table 5.5 Seasonal regression data extract—GDP

Quarter	GDP$2009	Time	Q1	Q2	Q3
1947 I	1934.471	1	1	0	0
1947 II	1932.281	2	0	1	0
1947 III	1930.315	3	0	0	1
1947 IV	1960.705	4	0	0	0

The Excel output for this model is given in Table 5.6.

Table 5.6 Regression output for seasonal GDP

SUMMARY OUTPUT

Regression Statistics	
Multiple R	0.983
R Square	0.966
Adjusted R Square	0.966
Standard Error	880.027
Observations	289

ANOVA

	Df	SS	MS	F	Significance F
Regression	4	6.33E+09	1.58E+09	2042.041	7.6E–208
Residual	284	2.2E+08	774447		
Total	288	6.55E+09			

	Coefficients	Standard Error	t Stat	P-value	Lower 95%	Upper 95%
Intercept	7.887	137.710	0.057	0.954	−263.173	278.948
Time	56.080	0.621	90.375	2.7E–211	54.8583	57.301
Q1	17.185	146.169	0.118	0.906	−270.528	304.897
Q2	5.785	146.676	0.039	0.969	−282.926	294.496
Q3	5.749	146.672	0.039	0.969	−282.954	294.451

Note that R Square increased from 0.965 in Table 5.2 to 0.966. Adjusted R Square rose the same amount, as there were few variables relative to observations. Note however that while Time is significant, none of the dummy variables are. The model is now:

$$\text{GDP} = 7.887 + 56.080 \times \text{Time} + \text{coefficient}$$
$$\text{of dummy variable per quarter}$$

The nice thing about this regression is that there is no error in guessing future variable values. The forecasts for 2018 are shown in Table 5.7.

The seasonal model has more content, and if there is significant seasonality can be much stronger than the trend model without seasonality. Here there is practically little difference (as we would expect, as the data was deseasonalized). Our intent here is simply to show how the method would work.

We can demonstrate error metrics with these forecasts. We limit ourselves to 1948s four quarterly observations to reduce space requirements. Table 5.8 shows calculations.

Absolute error is simply the absolute value of the difference between actual and forecast. Squared error squares this value (skipping applying the absolute function, which would be redundant). Absolute percentage

Table 5.7 Comparative forecasts

Time	Quarter	Time regression	Seasonal regression
287	II 2018	16,054	16,052
288	III 2018	16,110	16,108
289	IV 2018	16,166	16,159
290	I 2019	16,222	16,232

Table 5.8 Error calculations

Time	Actual	Time Reg	Abs error	Squared error	% Error
5	1989.535	295.529	1694.006	2,869,656	573.2
6	2021.851	351.609	1670.242	2,789,709	475.0
7	2033.155	407.688	1625.467	2,642,142	398.7
8	2035.329	463.768	1571.561	2,469,804	338.9

error divides absolute error by actual. The metric is the mean for each of these measures. In this case, the numbers are very high as can be seen in Figure 5.2 where the trend line is far below actual observations in 1948. The actual GDP has a clear nonlinear trend.

Software Demonstrations

For OLS regression, Excel was demonstrated earlier. The only limitation we perceive in using Excel is that Excel regression is limited to 16 independent variables. We can also use R for linear regression.

To install R, visit https://cran.rstudio.com/

Open a folder for R

Select Download R for windows

To install Rattle:
Open the R Desktop icon (32 bit or 64 bit) and enter the following command at the R prompt. R will ask for a CRAN mirror. Choose a nearby location.

>install.packages"(rattle)"

Enter the following two commands at the R prompt. This loads the Rattle package into the library and then starts up Rattle.

>library(rattle)

>rattle()

If the RGtk2 package has yet to be installed, there will be an error popup indicating that libatk–1.0–0.dll is missing from your computer. Click on the OK and then you will be asked if you would like to install GTK+. Click OK to do so. This then downloads and installs the appropriate GTK+ libraries for your computer. After this has finished, do exit from R and restart it so that it can find the newly installed libraries.

When running Rattle a number of other packages will be downloaded and installed as needed, with Rattle asking for the user's permission before doing so. They only need to be downloaded once.

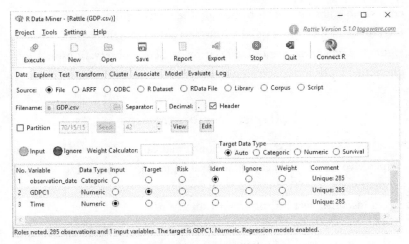

Figure 5.3 Rattle data-loading screenshot

Figure 5.3 shows an initial screen where we load the quarterly data file:

The data file is linked in the *Filename* menu. When we click on *Execute*, we see the data types. We select *Target* for GDPC1 as this is what we wish to predict. Note that we deselect the partition box—if we don't do that, Ratte will hold 30 percent of the data out for testing. While that is useful for some purposes, we don't want to do that here. Again, click on *Execute* to induce R to read GDP as the target. We now want to run a linear model. Click on the *Model* tab, yielding Figure 5.4.

R displays its options under linear models. Using the quarterly data, we select *Numeric* and *Linear*, and click on *Execute*. This yields the output shown in Figure 5.5.

Summary

There are many ways to extend time series. Moving average is one of the easiest, but can't forecast very far into the future. Regression models have been widely used in classical modeling. They continue to be very useful in data mining environments, which differ primarily in the scale of observations and number of variables used. Classical regression (usually OLS) can be applied to continuous data. Regression can be applied by conventional software such as SAS, SPSS, or EXCEL.R provides a linear model

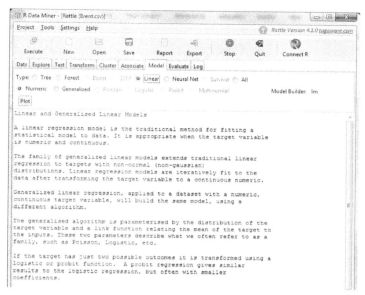

Figure 5.4 Linear regression screenshot

Figure 5.5 R linear model output—quarterly GDP

akin (but slightly different from) to OLS. There are many other forecasting methodologies, to include exponential smoothing. We covered the methods that relate to the techniques we will cover in future chapters. We have also initially explored the Brent crude oil data, demonstrating simple linear models and their output.

APPENDIX

Data Analysis Toolpak Add-In

Begin with Figure 5.6, and select File in the upper left corner.

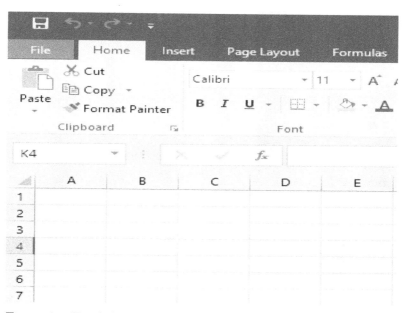

Figure 5.6 Excel sheet

This produces Figure 5.7.

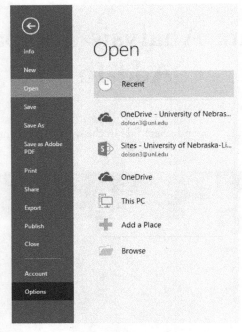

Figure 5.7 File results

Click on Options (bottom entry on menu—you get an Excel Options window—Figure 5.8). In the window, under Inactive Application Add-ins, select Analysis ToolPak.

Click on Add-ins on the left column and get Figure 5.9.

Make sure that Analysis ToolPak is selected, and click on the Go... button. That will give you the Data Analysis Tab (Figure 5.10), which includes Regression (used for both single and multiple regression) as well as correlation tools.

The Data tab is displayed in gray on the top bar in Figure 5.9—Data Analysis will be on far right on next row after you add-in. Note that this same window allows you to add-in SOLVER for linear programming.

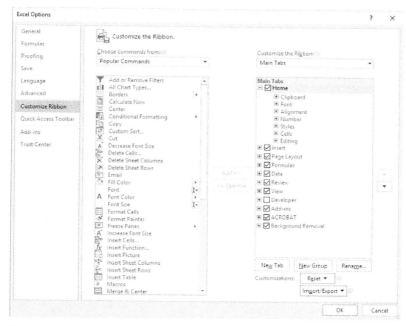

Figure 5.8 Excel options window

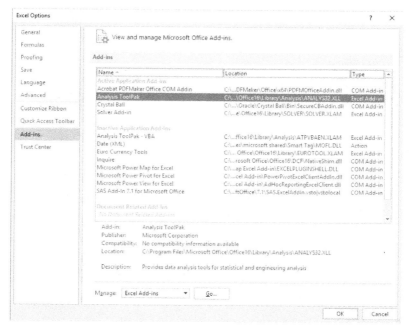

Figure 5.9 Select analysis toolPak

Figure 5.10 Data analysis tab

To Run Regression

You need to prepare the data by placing all independent variables in a contiguous block before you start—it is a good idea to have labels for each column at the top. Go to Data on the top ribbon, on the window you get select Data Analysis (Figure 5.11). Select Regression (you have to scroll down the menu):

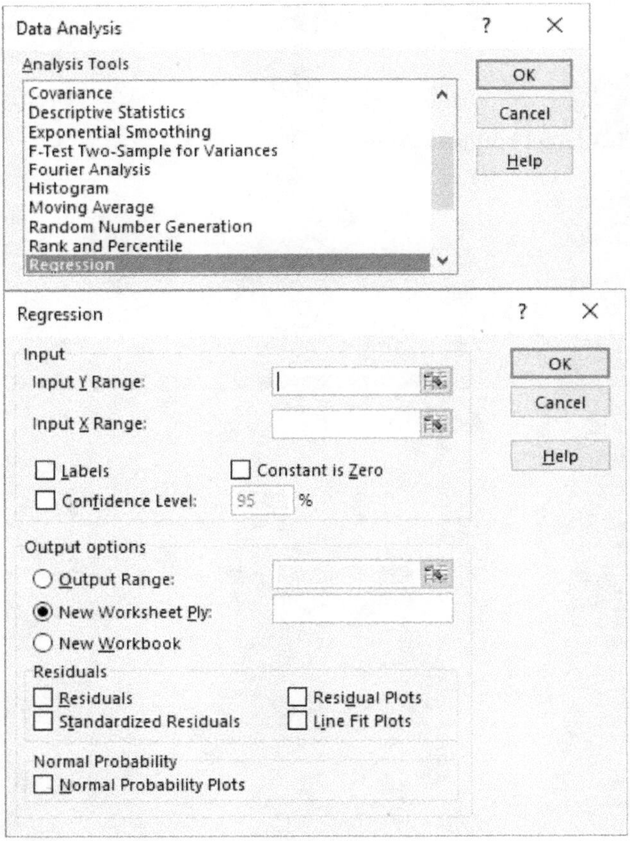

Figure 5.11 Regression windows

Enter the block for the dependent variable (X)

Enter the block for the independent variables (one or more Ys)

If you have labels, you need to click the Labels box.

You have choices of where to put the model

You obtain an OUTPUT SUMMARY (see Table 5.2 and others earlier in this chapter).

Usually it is best to place on a new worksheet, although you might want to place it on the same page you are working on.

To Run Correlation

Correlation is obtained as shown in Figure 5.12.

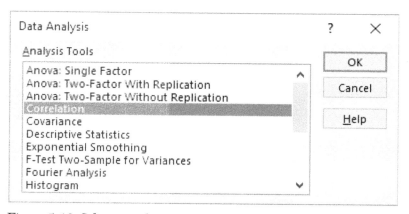

Figure 5.12 Select correlation

You get the window shown in Figure 5.13.

Enter the block of data (they have to be all numeric, although you can include column labels if you check the "Labels in First Row" box—highly recommended. You again have a choice of where to place the correlation matrix (a location on your current Excel sheet, or a new Excel sheet).

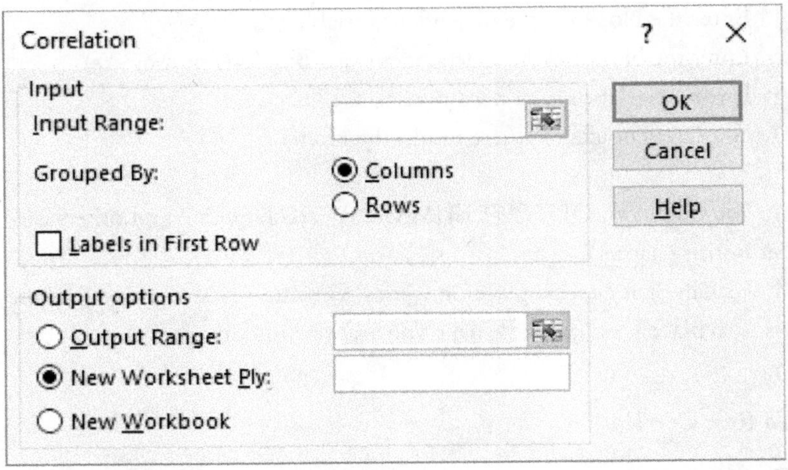

Figure 5.13 Correlation input window

CHAPTER 6

Multiple Regression

Regression models allow you to include as many independent variables as you want. In traditional regression analysis, there are good reasons to limit the number of variables. The spirit of exploratory data mining, however, encourages examining a large number of independent variables. Here we are presenting very small models for demonstration purposes. In data mining applications, the assumption is that you have very many observations, so that there is no technical limit on the number of independent variables.

Data Series

In Chapter 5 we covered simple regressions, using only time as an independent variable. Often we want to use more than one independent variable. Multiple ordinary least squares (OLS) regression allows consideration of other variables that might explain changes in what we are trying to predict. Here we will try to predict the Hang Sheng Shanghai (HIS) stock index, a major Chinese trading market. We consider five additional variables, with the intent of demonstrating multiple regression, not with the aim of completely explaining change in HSI. The variables we include the S&P 500 index of blue chip stocks in the United States, the New York Stock Exchange (NYSE) index of all stocks traded on that exchange, both reflecting U.S. capital performance, a possible surrogate for the U.S. economy, which has been closely tied to the Chinese economy over the time period considered. Eurostoxx is an index of European stocks, another Chinese trade partner. Each of these three stock indexes were obtained from http://finance.yahoo.com. Brent is the price of Brent crude oil, obtained from www.tradingeconomics.com/commodity/brent-crude-oil, reflecting a cost of doing business for Chinese industry as well as for the rest of the world. Brent crude oil price can be viewed as a reflection of risk, as its price is a key component of many costs, and this price has experienced radical changes. The last variable considered is the price of gold, which can be viewed as a measure of investor uncertainty (when things are viewed as really bad, investors often flee to gold). The gold data were obtained from http://goldprice.org/gold-price-history/html. All data used was monthly for the period January 2001 through April 2016.

We model the monthly price of the HangSeng index. Monthly data for the period January 1992 through December 2017 for six potential explanatory variables (NYSE index; S&P 500 index; T Rowe Price Euro index; Brent crude oil price; price of gold; time). A regression using all six variables yielded the time series regression shown in Table 6.1.

It can be seen from Table 6.1 that time has explained nearly 90 percent of the change in the index value. However, the series is quite volatile. This regression model is plotted against the MSCI in Figure 6.1, showing this volatility.

Many of the variables included probably don't contribute much, while others contribute a lot. An initial indicator is the p-value for each independent variable, shown in Table 6.1. P-values give an estimate of the probability that the beta coefficient is significant, which here specifically means is not zero or opposite in sign to what the model gives. In Table 6.1 the strongest fit is with NYSA and Gold, although S&P and Time also

Figure 6.1 Full model vs. actual HangSeng

Table 6.1 HangSeng monthly time series regression

SUMMARY OUTPUT					
Regression Statistics					
Multiple R	0.945				
R Square	**0.894**				
Adjusted R Square	**0.892**				
Standard Error	2036.909				
Observations	312				
ANOVA					
	df	*SS*	*MS*	*F*	*Significance F*
Regression	6	1.07E+10	1.78E+09	428.133	2.6E−145
Residual	305	1.27E+09	4148997		
Total	311	1.19E+10			

	Coefficients	*Standard Error*	*t Stat*	*P-value*	*Lower 95%*	*Upper 95%*
Intercept	115.202	671.560	0.172	0.864	−1206.28	1436.678
NYSE	**2.860**	0.372	7.684	**2.13E−13**	2.128	3.593
S&P	**−5.293**	1.438	−3.681	0	−8.122	−2.464
TRowPrEuro	**60.882**	65.225	0.933	0.351	−67.467	189.231
Brent	**−5.519**	10.752	−0.513	0.608	−26.675	15.638
Gold	**6.263**	0.817	7.665	**2.41E−13**	4.655	7.871
Time	**−16.494**	6.220	−2.652	**0.008**	−28.734	−4.254

have highly significant beta coefficients. Note the 0.95 confidence limit of the beta coefficients for TRowPrEuro and for Brent, which overlap zero, a demonstration of lack of significance. Table 6.2 selects these four variables in a second model.

This model loses some of its explanatory power (r-squared dropped from 0.894 to 0.888) but not much. (Adding an independent variable to a given set of regression independent variables must increase r-squared.) Thus we can conclude that dropping the TRowePrice Euro index and time had little to contribute. We do see that the *p*-values for Brent changed,

Table 6.2 Significant variable model

SUMMARY OUTPUT

Regression Statistics	
Multiple R	0.943
R Square	0.888
Adjusted R Square	0.887
Standard Error	2082.156
Observations	312

ANOVA

	df	SS	MS	F	Significance F
Regression	4	1.06E+10	2.65E+09	610.814	9.3E– 145
Residual	307	1.33E+09	4335373		
Total	311	1.19E+10			

	Coefficients	Standard Error	t Stat	P-value	Lower 95%	Upper 95%
Intercept	1671.120	355.044	4.707	3.81E– 06	972.494	2369.747
S&P	–3.954	1.424	–2.777	0.006	–6.755	–1.152
Brent	5.960	10.578	0.563	0.574	–14.854	26.774
NYSE	2.327	0.304	7.663	2.4E–13	1.729	2.924
Gold	3.993	0.597	6.690	1.06E– 10	2.819	5.167

now showing up as not significant. *P*-values are volatile and can change radically when independent variable sets are changed.

Even though Time was not significant in Table 6.1, it is a convenient independent variable by itself, because it is usually the only independent variable that can accurately be predicted in the future. Table 6.3 shows the output for a simple regression of the HangSeng versus only Time.

The beta coefficient given in Table 6.3 is the trend. Figure 6.2 shows this trend, as well as demonstrating why the r-squared dropped to 0.784. Note that here time is shown as highly significant (demonstrating how *p*-values can change across models):

Table 6.3 HangSeng regression vs. time

SUMMARY OUTPUT					
Regression Statistics					
Multiple R	0.886				
R Square	0.784				
Adjusted R Square	0.784				
Standard Error	2880.615				
Observations	312				

ANOVA

	df	SS	MS	F	Significance F
Regression	1	9.35E+09	9.35E+09	1126.909	2.9E–105
Residual	310	2.57E+09	8297944		
Total	311	1.19E+10			

	Coefficients	Standard Error	t Stat	P-value	Lower 95%	Upper 95%
Intercept	6507.564	326.951	19.904	2.3E–57	5864.24	7150.888
Time	60.784	1.811	33.569	2.9E–105	57.221	64.347

Figure 6.2 HangSeng time series

Correlation

Since we have multiple independent variable candidates, we need to consider first their strength of contribution to the dependent variable (Hang Sheng index), and second, overlap in information content with other independent variables. We want high correlation between Hang Sheng and the candidate independent variables. We want low correlation between independent variables. Table 6.4 provides correlations obtained from Excel.

The strongest relationship between the HangSeng index and candidate independent variables is with NYSE at 0.901, followed by Time (0.886), S&P (0.828), Gold (0.7998) and Brent (0.767). The TRowPrEuro index is lower (how low is a matter relative to the data set—here it is the weakest). Look at the r-score for Time and HangSeng (0.886). Square this and you get 0.785 (0.784 if you use the exact correlation value from Table 6.4 in Excel), which is the r-squared shown in Table 6.3. For a single independent variable regression, r-squared equals the r from correlation squared. Adding independent variables will always increase r-squared. To get a truer picture of the worth of adding independent variables to the model, adjusted R^2 penalizes the R^2 calculation for having extra independent variables.

Table 6.4 Correlations among variables

	Hang Seng	NYSE	S&P	TRow PrEuro	Brent	Gold
HangSeng	1.000					
NYSE	0.901	1.000				
S&P	0.828	0.964	1.000			
TRowPrEuro	0.450	0.624	0.644	1.000		
Brent	0.767	0.643	0.479	0.127	1.000	
Gold	0.799	0.677	0.610	0.023	0.840	1.000
Time	0.886	0.913	0.861	0.312	0.741	0.851

$$\text{Adjusted R}^2 = 1 - \frac{SSE(n-1)}{TSS(n-k)}$$

where SSE = sum of squared errors

MSR = sum of squared predicted values

TSS = SSE + MSR

n = number of observations

k = number of independent variables

Multiple Regression Models

We now need to worry about overlapping information content. The problem is multicollinearity, overlapping explanatory content of independent variables. The strongest correlation with HangSeng was with NYSE. But NYSE also has high correlations with all of the other candidate independent variables. While cutoffs are arbitrary, one rule of thumb might be to not combine independent variables that have more to do with each other than they do with the dependent variable. NYSE and time have more to do with each other than time does with HangSeng. You would expect NYSE and S&P to be highly correlated (they come from the same market), and S&P has a higher correlation with NYSE than with HangSeng. This relationship is true for all NYSE combinations. But we might be able to find sets of independent variables that fit our rule of thumb. Time and TRowPrEuro does, but TRowPrEuro had a relatively weak relationship with HangSeng. There are about six pairs of these independent variables that have less correlation with each other than each has with HangSeng. If we also require that cross-correlation of independent variables be below 0.5 (admittedly an arbitrary requirement), we eliminate Time/Brent and S&P/Gold. That leaves four pairs (we can't identify any triplets satisfying these restrictions, although in many data sets you can).

Time TRowPrEuro	r-squared 0.811	adjusted r-squared 0.819
S&P Brent	r-squared 0.863	adjusted r-squared 0.862
Brent TRowPrEuro	r-squared 0.714	adjusted r-squared 0.712
TRowPrEuro Gold	r-squared 0.825	adjusted r-squared 0.824

Of the two pairs we discarded because of mutual correlations over 0.5:

Time Brent   r-squared 0.811   adjusted r-squared 0.810
S&P Gold   r-squared 0.823   adjusted r-squared 0.822

We will retain the strongest of these (S&P and Brent crude oil), with regression output in Table 6.5.

The mathematical model is thus:

$$\text{HangSeng} = 2938.554 + 7.153 \times \text{S\&P} + 87.403 \times \text{Brent}$$

The p-value for the intercept doesn't really matter as we need an intercept in most cases. The p-values for the other two variables are all

Table 6.5 S&P and Brent regression

SUMMARY OUTPUT						
Regression Statistics						
Multiple R	0.929					
R Square	0.863					
Adjusted R Square	0.862					
Standard Error	2300.011					
Observations	312					

ANOVA					Significance	
	df	*SS*	*MS*	*F*	*F*	
Regression	2	1.03E+10	5.14E+09	972.464	4.7E–134	
Residual	309	1.63E+09	5290050			
Total	311	1.19E+10				

	Coefficients	*Standard Error*	*t Stat*	*P-value*	*Lower 95%*	*Upper 95%*
Intercept	2938.554	337.650	8.703	1.97E–16	2274.171	3602.938
S&P	7.153	0.287	24.905	7.36E–76	6.588	7.718
Brent	87.403	4.370	20.002	1.11E–57	78.805	96.001

Figure 6.3 Multiple regression vs. S&P and Brent

highly significant. Plotting this model vs. actual MSCI and its trend line is shown in Figure 6.3.

Clearly the multiple regression fits the data better than the trend. This is indicated quantitatively in the r-square (0.863) which has to be greater than the 0.784 r-squared of the simple regression vs. time. It is less than the r-squared of the full model (0.894), but the beta coefficients of this trimmed model should be much stabler than they were in the full model (the 95 percent limits for S&P on the full model were −8.122 to −2.464, while in the trimmed model they are 6.588 to 7.718, showing a reversal in sign!); Brent's 95 percent limits were −26.675 to 15.638, overlapping zero in the full model, and are a much stabler 78.805 to 96.001 in the trimmed model).

Using the model to forecast requires knowing (or guessing at) future independent variable values. A very good feature for Time is that there is no additional error introduced in estimating future time values.

$$\text{HangSeng} = 6507.564 + 60.784 \times \text{Time}$$

That is not the case for S&P or for Brent.

$$\text{HangSeng} = 2938.554 + 7.153 \times \text{S\&P} + 87.403 \times \text{Brent}$$

Table 6.6 Forecasts

Month	Time	S&P	Brent	TimeReg	MultReg
Jan 2018	313	2700	60	25533	27496
Feb 2018	314	2725	55	25594	27238
Mar 2018	315	2750	50	25655	26979
Apr 2018	316	2775	45	25715	26721
May 2018	317	2800	50	25776	27337
Jun 2018	318	2825	55	25837	27953

In Table 6.6 we guess at slight increases for both S&P and Brent values for the first six months of 2018, and compare forecasts for the simple time regression with the multiple regression model.

Note that we have to guess future values for S&P and Brent. If you monitor those series closely, you might have an educated guess, but there still is error that the regression model cannot measure. R-squared can only measure error over past observations. Still, it can provide a better model here, where the trend still lags a HangSeng high cycle seen in Figures 6.2 and 6.3.

Lagged Models

One way to avoid introducing extra error by guessing at future independent variable values is to use lags. This regresses the dependent variable against the independent variable values lagged by one or more periods. There usually is a loss of model fit, but at least there is no extra error introduced in the forecast from guessing at the independent variable values. Here we show the results of lagging S&P and Brent one, two, and three periods into the future. Table 6.7 shows the model for a lag of one period.

We can compare the three lagged models in Table 6.8 with their forecasts.

There is usually a tradeoff in lower fit (r-squared will usually drop) vs. the confidence of knowing the future independent variable values.

Table 6.7 Lag-1 model

Regression Statistics	
Multiple R	0.917792
R Square	0.842341
Adjusted R Square	0.841314
Standard Error	2440.704
Observations	310

ANOVA

	df	SS	MS	F	Significance F
Regression	2	9.77E+09	4.89E+09	820.1227	7.1E-124
Residual	307	1.83E+09	5957034		
Total	309	1.16E+10			

	Coefficients	Standard Error	t Stat	P-value	Lower 95%	Upper 95%
Intercept	3152.399	362.9181	8.686254	2.27E-16	2438.277	3866.521
S&PLag1	7.110527	0.313341	22.69265	1.27E-67	6.493961	7.727094
BrentLag1	85.43689	4.653736	18.35877	2.54E-51	76.27963	94.59414

Table 6.8 Lagged model results—S&P and Brent

Model	R^2	Intercept	S&P β	Brent β	Forecast 1	Forecast 2	Forecast 3
No Lag	0.863	2938.554	7.153	87.403			
Lag 1	0.842	3152.399	7.111	85.437	26377		
Lag 2	0.820	3335.7556	7.144	82.339	26468	26965	
Lag 3	0.799	3525.927	7.165	79.375	26542	27023	27791

Summary

Regression models have been widely used in classical modeling. They continue to be very useful in data mining environments, which differ primarily in the scale of observations and number of variables used.

Classical regression (usually ordinary least squares) can be applied to continuous data. Regression can be applied by conventional software such as SAS, SPSS, or EXCEL. The more independent variables, the better the fit. But for forecasting, the more independent variables, the more things that need to be identified (guessed at), adding to unmeasured error in the forecast.

There are many refinements to regression that can be accessed, such as stepwise linear regression. Stepwise regression uses partial correlations to select entering independent variables iteratively, providing some degree of automatic machine development of a regression model. Stepwise regression has its proponents and opponents, but is a form of machine learning.

CHAPTER 7

Logistic Regression

Logistic regression is a method of estimating the probability of an outcome for binary categorical variables. The variable of interest is often an event. The occurrence of this event is considered "success," and otherwise "failure." Examples include insurance claims being a fraud or legitimate, sales quote sent to a customer being successful or not, job applications succeed or not, and if age is a factor in tendency to buy a product or service. A simple example of one predictor for the outcome is a binary dependent variable and a continuous predictor. Similar to multiple linear regression, we may have multiple predictors including categorical variables, and a nominal or ordinal response variable. The next section gives a formal development of logistic regression. If you simply want to use logistic regression, you can glance through the material to get a general idea of what logistic regression does and proceed to your software. But if you want to know why, this material shows the mathematics behind it.

Odds of Dichotomous Events

Success or failure of a sales attempt depends on a number of factors including the customer income. Using annual income as the only predictor of sales will result in a model with one continuous variable and one categorical, dichotomous response. The sales attempt is either successful or fails, so we have only two possible outcomes. A linear regression model will have unrealistic results as it will have estimations of the response variable between the two possible values of success and failure. If values of one and zero assigned to the two levels of success and failure, a linear fit line also generates values beyond these two levels that are not meaningful. A transformation of probabilities based on observed frequencies of outcomes can lead to a logistic regression solution. We will assign zero and one as two levels of response variable, zero representing the "failure" outcome and "one" the success, as in Figure 7.1.

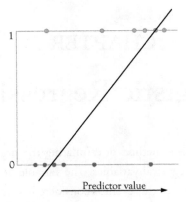

Figure 7.1 Linear fit

Probability of success in a binomial test is a conditional probability in which the value of dependent variable (y_i) is estimated based on the given values of a set of predictors (x_i). We can use the notation of $P(Y=y_i|x_1,...,x_n)$, given that Yi is the desired outcome, or one. Probability of success is calculated based on the relative frequency of this outcome among all observations:

$$P_{Success} = P(Y=1) = (\text{observed number of successes})/(\text{Total trials})$$

Since the total probability space for success and failure is one:

$$P_{Failure} = 1-P_{Success}$$

Odds of these events are calculated as the following. For simplicity we call probability of success "$P(x)$:"

$$\text{Odds}_{Success} = O(X) = \frac{\text{Probability of Success}}{\text{Probability of failure}} = \frac{P(x)}{1-p(x)}$$

$$\text{Odds}_{Failure} = \frac{1-P(x)}{1-(1-p(x))} = \frac{1-p(x)}{p(x)}$$

These equations are best represented by a sigmoid curve that estimates the odds of outcomes (Figure 7.2).

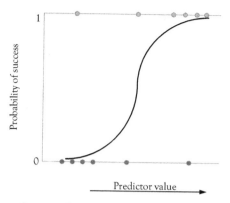

Figure 7.2 Sigmoid curve fit for likelihood

Log Transformation of Odds

A logarithmic transformation of odds function creates a linear model:

$$Ln(Odds_{Success}) = Ln\frac{P(x)}{1-p(x)} = Ln(P(x)) + Ln(1-p(x))$$

This linear model is represented in a general form of a linear function of one or more predictors, called Logit:

$$Ln(Odds_{Success}) = Ln(O(X)) = \beta_0 + \beta_1 x_1 + ... + \beta_n x_n$$

Solve the equation of "odds of success" for $P(x)$:

$$O(X) = \frac{P(x)}{1-p(x)} \Rightarrow O(X) - P[O(X)] = P(x) \Rightarrow [1+O(X)]\, P(x) = O(X) \Rightarrow$$

$$P(x) = \frac{o(x)}{1+o(x)} = \frac{1}{1+o(x)^{-1}}$$

Since $Ln(O(X)) = \beta_0 + \beta_1 x_1 + ... + \beta_n x_n$, then $O(X) = e^{\beta_0 + \beta_1 x_1 + ... + \beta_n x_n}$.
Replace the value of $O(x)$ in $P(x)$ function:

$$P(x) = \frac{1}{1+e^{-\beta_0 - \beta_1 x_1 - ... - \beta_n x_n}}$$

For a set of given $x_1, ..., x_n$ values the conditional probability of the set of given outcomes is given by the multiplication of all existing events, which are all probabilities of success, and all probabilities of failure. This product is called the likelihood function (L). The likelihood function must be maximized in order to find the optimum set of coefficients that generate the best fit to the data:

$$L = \prod_{y_{i=1}} p(x)_i \times \prod_{y_{i=0}} [1 - p(x)_i]$$

We can then transform the equation as follows:

$$L = \prod p(x_i)^{y_i} \times [1 - p(x_i)]^{1-y_i} \; y_i \in \{0,1\}$$

Log Likelihood Function

Taking the natural logarithm of both sides of the likelihood equation will generate the log-likelihood function. We will maximize this function instead of the likelihood function. Logarithm is a monotonic function. Increasing values of a variable will generate increasing logarithms of those values and decreasing values of the original data will result in decreasing values of logarithms. Finding the maximum value of a log-transformed data will match the maximum point of the original data. Maximizing the values of the log-likelihood function requires the same coefficients of the variables as the original values.

Log likelihood function $= Ln(L) = Ln\{\prod P(x_i)^{y_i} \times [1 - P(x_i)]^{1-y_i}\}$

$$Ln(L) = Ln\{[P(x_i)^{y_i}] + Ln\{[1 - P(x_i)]^{1-y_i}\}$$

$$Ln(L) = \sum_{i=1}^{n} y_i Ln(p(x_i)) + (1 - y_i)Ln(1 - p(x_i))$$

$$Ln(L) = \sum_{i=1}^{n} y_i Ln\left(\frac{1}{1 + e^{-\beta_0 - \beta_1 x_1 - \dots - \beta_n x_n}}\right) - (1 - y_i)Ln\left(\frac{e^{-\beta_0 - \beta_1 x_1 - \dots - \beta_n x_{n1}}}{1 + e^{-\beta_0 - \beta_1 x_1 - \dots - \beta_n x_n}}\right)$$

$$Ln(L) = \sum_{i=1}^{n} y_i \left[Ln\left(\frac{1}{1 + e^{-\beta_0 - \beta_1 x_1 - \dots - \beta_n x_n}}\right) - Ln\left(\frac{e^{-\beta_0 - \beta_1 x_1 - \dots - \beta_n x_{n1}}}{1 + e^{-\beta_0 - \beta_1 x_1 - \dots - \beta_n x_n}}\right) \right] +$$

$$Ln\left(\frac{e^{-\beta_1 x_1 - \dots - \beta_n x_{n1}}}{1 + e^{-\beta_0 - \beta_1 x_1 - \dots - \beta_n x_n}}\right)$$

A simple form of this equation for one predictor is:

$$\text{Ln(L)} = \sum_{i=1}^{n} y_i \left[\text{Ln}\left(\frac{1}{1+e^{-\beta_0-\beta_1 x}}\right) - \text{Ln}\left(\frac{e^{-\beta_0-\beta_1 x}}{1+e^{-\beta_0-\beta_1 x}}\right) \right] + \text{Ln}\left(\frac{e^{-\beta_0-\beta_1 x}}{1+e^{-\beta_0-\beta_1 x}}\right)$$

$\text{Ln(A)} - \text{Ln(B)} = \text{Ln(A/B)}$. We apply this rule to the subtraction of natural logarithms and summarize the last term by multiplying the numerator and denominator by "$e^{\beta_0+\beta_1 x}$". The log likelihood function will summarize further to the following:

$$\text{Ln(L)} = \sum_{i=1}^{n} y_i [\text{Ln}(e^{\beta_0+\beta_1 x})] + \text{Ln}\left(\frac{1}{1+e^{\beta_0+\beta_1 x}}\right)$$

Based on the natural logarithm definition we have $\text{Ln}(e^{\beta_0+\beta_1 x}) = \beta_0 + \beta_1 x$ which leads to the following steps:

$$\text{Ln(L)} = \sum_{i=1}^{n} y_i (\beta_0 + \beta_1 x) + \text{Ln}\left(\frac{1}{1+e^{\beta_0+\beta_1 x}}\right)$$

$$\text{Ln(L)} = \sum_{i=1}^{n} y_i (\beta_0 + \beta_1 x) - \text{Ln}(1 + e^{\beta_0+\beta_1 x})$$

Similarly, we can expand this equation for multiple predictors as the following:

$$\text{Ln(L)} = \sum_{i=1}^{n} y_i (\beta_0 + \beta_1 x_1 + \dots + \beta_n x_n) - \text{Ln}(1 + e^{\beta_0+\beta_1 x_1 + \dots + \beta_n x_n})$$

Maximizing the log-likelihood function requires optimal coefficients of a simple or multiple logistic regression. We will use Excel solver for optimization of coefficients to demonstrate all steps of the solution.

Simple and Multiple Logistic Regression

Sale file demonstrates 200 records of calls made through a sales promotion to a customer list. The response variable Sale is the outcome of the call. Successful calls where the customer agreed to buy the product are marked "1" and otherwise "0." Independent variables in this file are "Income," showing the annual household income in thousands of dollars, "Household" showing the number of household residents, and "Call" showing the call duration in seconds. The manager's understanding is that customers with higher income, having a larger number of household residents, and staying longer on phone are more likely to eventually buy the product. Our objective is to determine the optimal coefficients of a logit function that will maximize the log likelihood of success, "Sale."

For a simple logistic regression, we will consider only "Income" as the predictor of "Sale." Cells H1 and H2 in the Excel worksheet are reserved for decision variables of maximization, the constant value and coefficient of predictor in likelihood function (L). Two small values entered as initial numbers to start the optimization.

Log-Likelihood formula for the first row of data is entered in cell C2:

$$Ln(L) = \sum_{i=1}^{n} y_i (\beta_0 + \beta_1 x) - Ln(1 + e^{\beta_0 + \beta_1 x})$$

Excel formula is as follows. All references to decision variables (H1 and H2) must be absolute since we will copy this formula down in column C for all observations:

=A2*($H$1+$H$2*B2)-LN(1+EXP($H$1+$H$2*B2))

Figure 7.3 shows how this looks in Excel.

Calculate the sum of all numbers of column C in cell C203:=SUM(C2:C201)

This value is the total likelihood of all outcomes, the value we try to maximize by changing decision variables in cells H1 and H2. Start values of both decision variables are 0.001. Use the Excel solver tool for this optimization. Objective cell is the total log-likelihood, cell C203 and changing cells are H1 and H2. Solving method is generalized reduced gradient (GRG) as it is a method capable of solving nonlinear problems.

	A	B	C	D	E	F	G	H
1	Sale	Income	Ln(L)				β_0	0.0001
2	0	35.122	=A2*($H$1+$H$2*B2)-LN(1+EXP($H$1+$H$2*B2))				β_1	0.0001
3	1	41.338	=A3*($H$1+$H$2*B3)-LN(1+EXP($H$1+$H$2*B3))					
4	0	29.802	=A4*($H$1+$H$2*B4)-LN(1+EXP($H$1+$H$2*B4))					
5	1	36.872	=A5*($H$1+$H$2*B5)-LN(1+EXP($H$1+$H$2*B5))					
6	0	31.522	=A6*($H$1+$H$2*B6)-LN(1+EXP($H$1+$H$2*B6))					

Figure 7.3 Excel worksheet for simple logistic regression

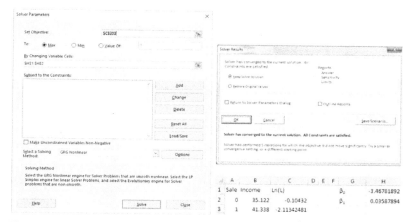

	A	B	C	D	E	F	G	H
1	Sale	Income	Ln(L)			β_0		-3.46781892
2	0	35.122	-0.10432			β_1		0.03587894
3	1	41.338	-2.11342481					

Figure 7.4 Solver input interface, the results screen, and optimized values for β_0 and β_1

Remove the default check on "Make Unconstrained Variables Non-Negative" and click on "Solve." Solver results screen appears with "Keep Solver Solution" checked. Click on OK to keep the values (Figure 7.4).

The logistic equation will be: $Ln(O(X)) = \beta_0 + \beta_1 x_1$ or $O(X) = e^{\beta_0 + \beta_1 x_1} = e^{-3.4678 + 0.0358789X}$

For example the odds of purchasing for a household with annual $60,000 income will be:

$$O(X) = e^{-3.4678 + 0.0358789(60)} = 0.2684$$

Probability of purchasing, $P(x) = \dfrac{1}{1 + O(x)^{-1}} = \dfrac{1}{1 + 0.2684^{-1}} = 0.21$

Calculating R^2 and Predictor Coefficient Significance

Goodness of fit tests are necessary for statistical tests including the logistic regression model. R^2 in linear regression models determines the extent in which variations of dependent variable are explained by variations of the independent variable. For a binary logistic regression model R^2 is calculated by the following formula:

$$R^2_{Logit} = \frac{-2MLn(L)_{Null} - (-2MLn(L)_{Model})}{-2MLn(L)_{Null}}$$

$MLn(L)_{Model}$ = Maximum Log-Likelihood of the model with all parameters
$MLn(L)_{Null}$ = Maximum Log-Likelihood of the model when the predictor
    coefficient is zero

Tests of significance compare the models with estimated coefficients of predictors, and coefficients of zero in order to determine if the estimated coefficient as the slope of a line makes a significant difference comparing to when it is zero. A zero coefficient represents no relationship between the dependent and independent variables.

For the simple logistic regression problem of sales and income, we have already calculated $MLn(L)_{Model}$. Repeating the optimization process with coefficient $\beta_1 = 0$ will calculate the maximum log-likelihood without the predictor. The goal is to compare the outcome and see if adding the predictor makes a significant difference in the outcome, and how the model explains variations of the dependent variable. In case of observing a significant difference between the two models, the independent variable is a significant predictor of the response. Set the predictor coefficient value to zero in cell H2. Use Excel solver and set the changing variable cell as H1 only. This is the only change from the previous solution (see Figure 7.5).

Running the Excel solver will generate the following results:

$$\beta_0 = -0.6856565$$

$$MLn(L)_{Null} = -127.5326$$

Full model $MLn(L)_{Model}$ was previously calculated as -109.7608. Using the R^2 formula:

$$R^2_{Logit} = \frac{-2(-127.5326) - 2(-109.7608)}{-2(-127.5326)} = 0.13935$$

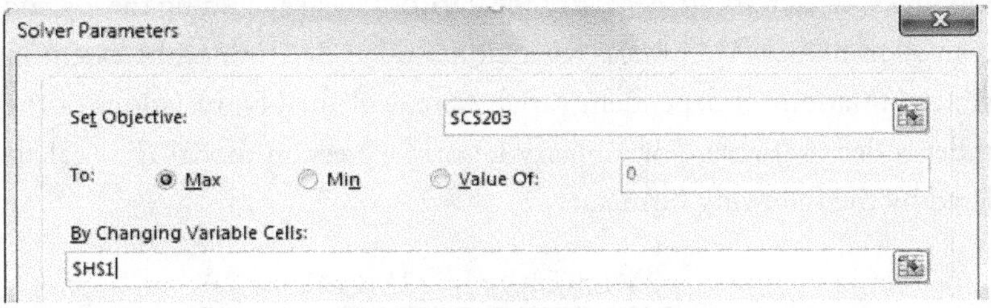

Figure 7.5 Solver set up for null model calculating $MLn(L)_{Null}$

Test of significance for predictor variable Sale, is a likelihood ratio test. This test compares the likelihoods of the full and null model in obtaining results that are not significantly different. The likelihood ratio is calculated by the following formula:

$$\text{Likelihood Ratio} = -2\text{Ln}\frac{\text{Likelihood for Null Model}}{\text{Likelihood for alternative (Full) Model}} = -2\text{Ln}(L)_{\text{Null}} + 2\text{Ln}(L)_{\text{Model}}$$

The likelihood ratio for the current problem is calculated as: $-2(-127.5326)+2(-109.7608)=35.54$

The likelihood ratio distribution is close to χ^2 so a χ^2 test can determine the significance of the parameter elimination of this model. If the null and original models do not make a significant difference, the parameter is not a good predictor of the outcome. Degrees of freedom for the χ^2 test equals the number of parameters eliminated from the model. Here it is one. An Excel function can directly calculate the p-value of this χ^2 test:

P = CHISQ.DIST.RT(Likelihood_Ratio, 1) = CHISQ.DIST.RT(35.54, 1) = 2.49E– 09

This small p-value indicates that Income is a significant predictor of sales.

Misclassification Rate

In a copy of the worksheet calculate the estimated probability of success (Sale) for each given income $P(X)= \dfrac{1}{1+e^{-\beta_0-\beta_1 x}}$. Excel formula for the first row in column H is: =1/(1+EXP(−$G$1 − B2*$G$2)). Copying this formula in column H as demonstrated in Figure 7.5 calculates probabilities for all observations. Any probability smaller than 0.5 is assigned to failure (0) and otherwise success (1). Excel logical function IF can be used to do this in column I:

=IF(H2<0.5, 0, 1)

We can also calculate the correct and misclassification rates. If an observation is "0" or "1" and estimated correctly, we can assign "1" to this outcome and if the classification is wrong comparing to the observed outcome, "0." Use Excel function IF and logical arguments to compare

H	I	J	K	L	M
P(X)	Estimated Outcome	Clasification			
=1/(1+EXP(-$G$1-B2*$G$2))	=IF(H2<0.5,0,1)	=IF(OR(AND(A2=0, H2<0.5), AND(A2=1, H2>=0.5)),1,0)		Correct classification	=SUM(J2:J201)/200
=1/(1+EXP(-$G$1-B3*$G$2))	=IF(H3<0.5,0,1)	=IF(OR(AND(A3=0, H3<0.5), AND(A3=1, H3>=0.5)),1,0)		Misclassification	=1-M2
=1/(1+EXP(-$G$1-B4*$G$2))	=IF(H4<0.5,0,1)	=IF(OR(AND(A4=0, H4<0.5), AND(A4=1, H4>=0.5)),1,0)			

Figure 7.6 Correct and misclassification rates

values in column J by the following formula for the first row and copy for all observations:

=IF(OR(AND(A2=0, H2<0.5), AND(A2=1, H2>=0.5)),1,0)

The sum of all numbers in this column represents the number of correct classifications. The correct classification rate is the ratio of this number to 200, the number of observations. The misclassification rate is the complement of this rate. Correct classification is calculated by this formula: =SUM(J2:J201)/200 =0.705 and misclassification rate is 1– 0.705 =0.295 (Figure 7.6).

Multiple Logistic Regression

Multiple logistic regression solution follows a similar method as simple regression. There are a few differences because of the number of variables exist in the model. In the data worksheet reserve four decision variables for the constant and three coefficients of predictors as demonstrated in Figure 7.6. Using the Sales file with all three predictors, the general formula of Log-Likelihood is:

$$Ln(L)= \sum_{i=1}^{n} y_i (\beta_0 + \beta_1 x_1 + ... + \beta_n x_n) - Ln(1 + e^{\beta_0 + \beta_1 x_1 + ... + \beta_n x_n})$$

We can implement this formula in Excel for the first row of observations as:

Ln(L)=A6*($B$1+$B$2*B6+$B$3*C6+$B$4*D6) – LN(1+EXP ($B$1+$B$2*B6+$B$3*C6+$B$4*D6))

After copying this formula into column E for all observations and summation of log likelihoods in cell H1 we can start Excel Solver. Initial

Figure 7.7 Worksheet and solver set up for multiple logistic regression

values of decision variables are 0.001. Solver solution method is GRG (Figure 7.7).

Optimum coefficients are calculated as: $\beta_0 = -4.47$, $\beta_1 = 0.035$, $\beta_2 = 0.2434$, $\beta_3 = -0.00018$

For example the probability of a household with annual income of $60,000, five residents, and staying on promotion call for 100 seconds is calculated based by the following formula:

$$P(X) = \frac{1}{1 + e^{-\beta_0 - \beta_1 x_1 - \beta_2 x_2 - \beta_3 x_3}}$$

$$P(X) = \frac{1}{1 + e^{[4.47 - 0.035(60) - 0.2434(5) + 0.00018(100)]}} = 0.2367$$

After determining the coefficients of predictors we set the values of all predictor coefficients to zero in order to run the Solver and obtain the value of $MLn(L)_{Null}$. This is one of the components of R^2. Excel Solver changing cell will be "B1" only. This value is calculated using the following formula:

$$R^2_{Logit} = \frac{-2MLn(L)_{Null} - (-2MLn(L)_{Model})}{-2MLn(L)_{Null}} = (-2*H1 - (-2*H2))/(-2*H1) = 0.1553$$

The significance of each variable in this model is tested by a similar method as the simple logistic regression. The decision variable (coefficient) for that variable is set to zero in a Solver run, and then a χ^2 test on the likelihood ratio will determine the significance of the variable. For

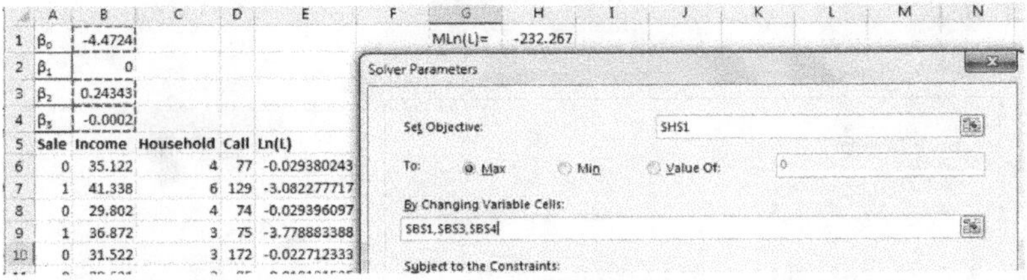

Figure 7.8 Solver and worksheet setup for testing the significance of income

example the setup for testing the significance of Income is as demonstrated in Figure 7.8.

This is a reduced model and after optimization its MLn(L) is calculated as −124.41. Maximum log-likelihood of the full model is already calculated as −107.722, so the likelihood ratio is: −2(−124.41)+ 2(−107.722)=33.3787.

The χ^2 test p-value with "one" degree of freedom, the number of eliminated variables, is:

$$P= CHISQ.DIST.RT(33.3787, 1)= 7.58E- 09.$$

The conclusion is that Income is a significant predictor of Sales. Following a similar process for Household and Call, their P-values are 0.0461 and 0.96 respectively. These p-values determine that the number of household residents is also a significant predictor at alpha level of 5%, but call duration is not a significant predictor in this model. The correct and misclassification rates are calculated using the base formulas of simple logistic regression and adding the other predictors.

$$P(X)=1/(1+EXP(-\$B\$1-\$B\$2*B6-\$B\$3*C6-\$B\$4*D6))$$

Software Solution for Logistic Regression

We will demonstrate use of Rattle to obtain a logistic regression model for the data file we have been using (SaleData.csv, converted to comma separated variables for Rattle). We covered loading Rattle in Chapter 5 (Figure 5.3). We can also show how Rattle models this data. Figure 7.9

Figure 7.9 Loading SaleData.csv in Rattle

shows loading the data file (note that the Partition box needs to be unclicked, and then the Execute button clicked on):

Here we want the dependent variable to be Sale, which is a 0/1 variable (sale or not). There are three independent variables (Income, Household, and Call, described earlier). We can now click on the Model tab, yielding Figure 7.10 showing the Rattle modeling screen.

Given that the dependent variable is 0/1, Rattle will assume you want a logistic regression model. The model is run by clicking on the Execute button on the top row of Figure 7.10, yielding the multiple regression output in Figure 7.11.

Thus logistic regression can be supported by multiple softwares. Rattle is far easier to run than the manipulations needed in Excel. But this chapter has provided mathematical presentation of logistic regression for those students interested in knowing why it works.

Summary

Logistic regression is a highly useful tool when the dependent variable is dichotomous (either/or; yes/no; 0–1). It is a linear regression, but over data that is transformed to a nonlinear function. This is a very important tool in data mining, where many applications involve classification of

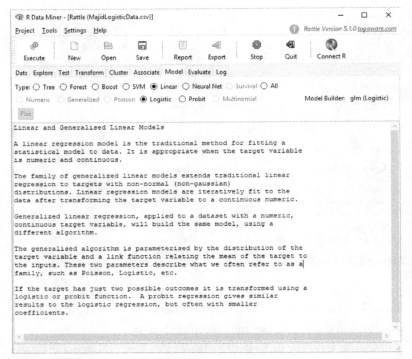

Figure 7.10 Rattle logistic regression modeling screen

cases, to include fraud detection in insurance, prediction of bank loan default, or customer profiling in marketing, with the intent of identifying potential customer profiles worth sending expensive promotional materials. It can be extended to more than two outcomes as well, as in human resources classification of employees, or refinements of any of the dichotomous cases cited earlier.

This chapter has shown how logistic regression can be accomplished on Excel. There are many other software products that provide this support as well, to include R and R's interface open source software Rattle.

Figure 7.11 Rattle multiple logistic regression model output

CHAPTER 8

Linear Programming

Business analytics refers to the use of quantitative analysis to support managerial decision making. It is concerned with the process of managerial decision making, as well as the tools used to support it (management science). This chapter seeks to explain the importance of optimization in business, demonstrate how linear programming (LP) models can be constructed, and show how they can be solved using *Solver* in *Excel*. The assumptions of LP models are discussed as well as model complications. Special model types are demonstrated, to include zero-one, transportation, and assignment models.

Optimization

LP is a particular type of mathematical programming. Mathematical programming has been used to improve the efficiency of many business operations. The following vignette hopefully demonstrates some of the potential of optimization models to better organizational management. LP is one of the most powerful analytic tools available to support operations management. LP provides the optimal, or best possible, solution to problems that can be formulated by a linear function subject to a set of linear constraints. This has proven extremely useful in many operations management applications, some of which are described in Table 8.1.

LP provides means of modeling these and other important operations management problems in order to identify more efficient methods of doing business. While LP provides a great deal of benefit, it comes with a fairly high price, in that only certain types of decision problems can be appropriately modeled with LP. This usually involves allocation of limited resources to alternative uses. The biggest drawbacks to this very powerful technique are that the decision problem must be expressed in linear functions, and since the very best possible solution is sought, minor

Table 8.1 Typical linear programming models

Type of model	Variables	Function to optimize	Typical constraints
Product mix	Number of products to 7produce	Maximize contribution to profit	Resource limits, such as time, labor, material; Maximum or minimum quantities
Blending	Amount of materials to combine to produce one unit of product	Minimize cost	Resource limits; Demand requirements
Production line scheduling	Sequence of production	Minimize cost	Resource limits; Time requirements
Inventory	Number of inventory items to order by period	Minimize cost (sum of production and inventory)	On-hand minimums by time period; Inventory balance equations
Transportation	Assign sources for distribution of goods to demands	Minimize cost	Capacity limits at sources; Demand requirements
Assignment	Assign sources of resources to tasks	Minimize cost	Conventionally sources and demand capacities equal 1

changes in assumed coefficient values can have a drastic impact upon the resulting solution.

Demonstration Model

To demonstrate LP, we will use a simplified problem involving identification of a company's optimal product mix. This small canning company specializes in gourmet canned foods. They can five combinations of ham, lima beans, and jalapeno peppers. Their five products are listed in the following. Marketing's estimated maximum daily demands are given in terms of cans (each of which contain 16 ounces by weight). Marketing has also made commitments in the form of signed contracts to deliver. The maximum demands include these signed contract commitments (Table 8.2).

The production department obtains input materials and fills 16 ounce cans. All quantities are in ounces, all costs and sales prices/can are in $.

Table 8.2 *Problem data*

Product	Max demand (16 oz. cans) (includes signed contracts)	Signed contracts/day (minimum demands)
Ham and beans	10000 cans/day	5000 cans/day
Jalapeno ham and beans	4000 "	1000 "
Lima beans	6000 "	1000 "
Jalapeno lima beans	4000 "	2000 "
Jalapeno peppers	1000 "	0 (new product)

Table 8.3 *Data per Can*

Product	Ham	Lima beans	Jalapenos	Water	Canning cost	Sales price
Ham and beans	4	9	0	3	0.05	2.31
Jalapeno ham and beans	3	9	1	3	0.05	2.00
Lima beans	0	14	0	2	0.05	0.85
Jalapeno lima beans	0	12	1	3	0.05	0.90
Jalapeno peppers	0	0	12	4	0.05	1.35
Cost of materials	0.40/oz	0/05/oz	0.10/oz	free		

There is a maximum production limit of 24,000 cans/day. Canning costs are constant. Requirements by can type are given in the following. It costs the company five cents to process each can. Current sales price is given in the last column of Table 8.3.

The company has a contract with a ham supplier for daily delivery of up to 30,000 ounces of ham at $0.30 per ounce. They also have a contract with a lima bean supplier for up to 100,000 ounces of lima beans per day at $0.05 per ounce. They do not have to pay for materials they do not use. They grow their own jalapenos, which cost $0.10 per ounce to pick (shown previously). There is more jalapeno supply than can be used. There is also an unlimited supply of tangy bayou water.

Components

LP models consist of variables, functions in terms of these variables, and limits to functions. To build a LP model of a decision problem, it is usually easiest to concentrate upon the decision to be made. Those things that are within decision maker control are usually the appropriate decision variables. In the canning case, the decision is how many cans of each product to produce each day. Another element that often helps the modeler is to identify the objective of the decision. Usually, that will be profit. The variables are those problem elements within decision maker control that contribute to profit. If there is difficulty identifying decision variables, sometimes thinking about how profit can be measured helps that identification. The last element of the model is the set of limits to the decision. Mathematical programming is very flexible in allowing the modeler to impose limits to the decision. It is possible to limit the decision so much that there is no possible way to satisfy all the limits (infeasibility). If that happens, the crux of the decision will be what limits have to be released. The reverse case is where important limits are left out. If the resulting model solution seems impractical, the outrageous features of the solution provide clues as to missing limits (Table 8.4).

Variables: The decision variables here are the number of cans to produce daily (H&B, JHB, LB, JLB, and JP). Variables, as the name implies, are allowed to take on different values. Some LP models require specific variables to take on specified values, either integer, or 0–1. As far as modeling is concerned, this is no problem; simply specify which variables have which restrictions. Requirements for integer or 0–1 variables may involve significant problems for solution in large models, but this can be left to the computer.

Functions: Functions are mathematical statements measuring something in terms of the variables. Profit is an example of a function. Variables can be included in the model to represent function levels, such as the variables HAM, BEANS, and CANS in the demonstration model. In order to measure a functional value, we must know the rate of contribution of each variable unit to the function. In the case of profit, we need to know how much profit the company can expect from each can, by product. The profit function was developed in the following table, yielding

Table 8.4 *Canning model parameters*

	Product	Min cans/ day	Max cans/ day	Sales price	Ham	Beans	Peppers	Can	Profit
H&B	Ham and beans	5000	10000	2.31	-4x0.4	-9x0.05		-0.05	=0.21
JHB	Jalapeno H&B	1000	4000	2.00	-3x0.4	-9x0.05	-1x0.02	-0.05	=0.20
LB	Lima beans	1000	6000	0.85		-14x0.05		-0.05	=0.10
JLB	Jalapeno lima beans	2000	4000	0.90		-12x0.05	-1x0.01	-0.05	=0.15
JP	Jalapeno peppers	0	1000	1.35			-12x0.01	-0.05	=0.10

Profit = 0.21 H&B + 0.20 JHB + 0.10 LB + 0.15 JLB + 0.10 JP

Functions can be limited to form constraints. Constraints can be equalities (=), less than or equal relationships (≤), or greater than or equal relationships (≥). Contracts have been signed to provide a minimum number of cans by product. The LP model can be constrained to force those minimum levels to be met by the solution. One constraint would be required for each variable with a minimum level of attainment. The function in this case would simply be the limited variable.

H&B	≥	5000
JHB	≥	1000
LB	≥	1000
JLB	≥	2000

The same can be done to limit the decision to stay at or below maximum demand levels.

H&B	≤	10000
JHB	≤	4000
LB	≤	6000
JLB	≤	4000
JP	≤	1000

Resource limitations can be included, such as the amount of ham and lima beans available. In this case, we can create new variables to measure key quantities.

HAM	≤	30000
BEANS	≤	100000
CANS	≤	24000
HAM	=	4 H&B + 3 JHB
BEANS	=	9 H&B + 9 JHB + 14 LB + 12 JLB
CANS	=	1 H&B + 1 JHB + 1 LB + 1 JLB + 1 JP

We can also create a variable to measure other items of interest.

PEPPERS   =1 JHB+ 1 JLB + 12 JP

A major benefit of LP is the ability to impose any limit on the model, as long as the limits include only linear functions.

Solution

Models in EXCEL can be optimized with *Solver*, which allows you to find optimal solutions to constrained optimization problems formulated as spreadsheet models. (Check the list of available add-ins under *Tools/Add-Ins*. If *Solver* is not listed, you will have to reinstall Excel, using a custom installation, or in the case of Office 2000 selecting *Add-Ins* and checking *Solver*.)

To use *Solver*, you should design your spreadsheet to include the following:

1. A cell for each decision variable,
2. A cell that calculates the objective function value,
3. Cells for each constraint function,
4. A cell for each function limit.

It is usually convenient to lay out your variables in rows or columns and provide descriptive labels either to the left of the columns or above the rows; this improves the readability and manageability of your models.

In *Solver*, decision variables are called *adjustable cells*, or *changing cells*; and the objective function cell is called the *target cell*. *Solver* identifies values of the changing cells that minimize or maximize the target cell value. *Solver* is easier to use if you define a cell for each of the constraint functions in your model (that is, the left-hand-sides of the constraints). For example, in the canning problem example, the following spreadsheet would model the problem (Table 8.5).

The spreadsheet contains the listing of the decision variables in cells A2 through A6. The variable cells themselves are B2 through B6. The target cell is the profit function, cell C7. The input data is found in columns C through G, rows two through six. Row seven contains functions. The variable CANS is simply the sum of the five decision variables (SUM(B2:B6)). SUMPRODUCT is a useful EXCEL function

Table 8.5 Excel worksheet for model

	A	B	C	D	E	F	G
1	Product	Quantity	Profit	HAM	BEANS	Min	Max
2	H&B		0.21	4	9	5,000	10,000
3	JHB		0.2	3	9	1,000	4,000
4	LB		0.1		14	1,000	6,000
5	JLB		0.15		12	2,000	4,000
6	JP		0.1			0	1,000
7	CANS	=SUM(B2:B6)	=SUMPRO-DUCT($B$2:$B$6,C2:C6)	=SUMPRO-DUCT($B$2:$B$6,D2:D6)	=SUMPRO-DUCT($B$2:$B$6,E2:E6)		
8	Limits	24,000		30,000	100,000		

that makes it easy to multiply one vector times another. In this case, the vector of decision variable values (B2:B6) is multiplied by the coefficients in columns B (for cans), C (for profit), D (for ham) and E (for beans). Constraint limits are found in row eight.

Solver

The next step is to activate *Solver*, an add-in to Excel that can be used to solve mathematical programming models. To add-in *Solver*, you need to click on Excel's options heading on the left of the initial screen. This presents a window, on the left of which is another list, the second from the bottom of which is "Add-ins" which you should select. This presents yet another window with a menu of Add-ins available. The fourth of those should be "Solver Add-in" which you should select, after which you click on the "Go…" button at the bottom of this window. That should add-in *Solver*. Now open a file, and at the top list of options is a "Data" button. If you click on that, at the far right *Solver* should appear. If that is selected, you obtain the window shown in Figure 8.1.

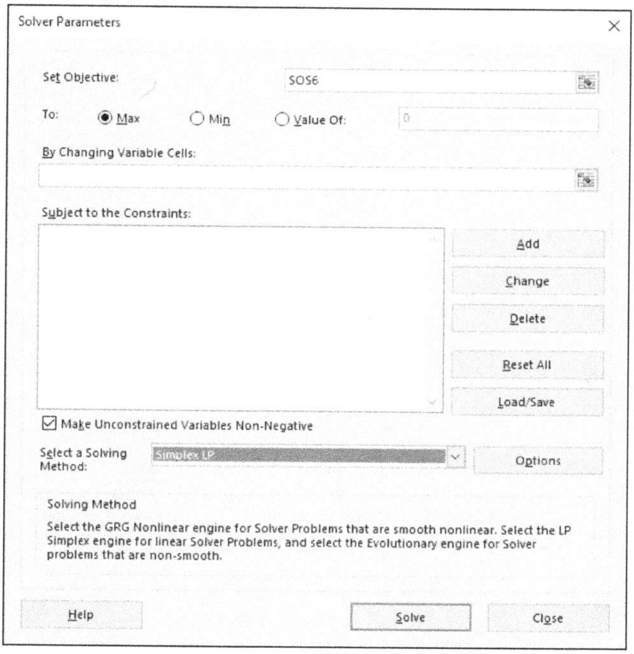

Figure 8.1 Initial Solver window

For the model in Table 8.5, we left the cursor on cell C7, the target cell. $C$7 will be in the target cell box because that is where we left the cursor. If you want another cell, this can be changed. The default is to maximize this function. The function can be minimized by clicking on that radio button, or a specific target value can be sought with the third radio button. We have filled in the next box, specifying which cells on the spreadsheet can be changed (the variables—cells B2:B6). The next step is to add the constraints. This is accomplished by clicking on the ADD button, once for each constraint. We need constraints to limit ham, limit beans, limit cans, stay at or above minimums, and stay at or below maximums. We also usually need to specify that each variable must not be negative, although the minimums by product take care of that here. Figure 8.2 shows the model.

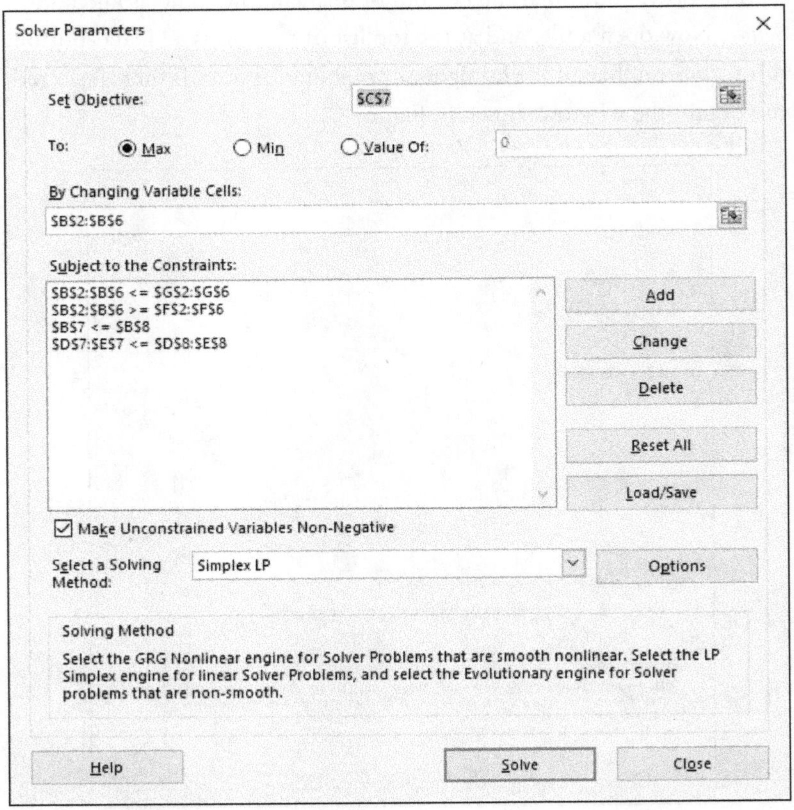

Figure 8.2 Solver model entered

Each of the decision variables is specified to be less than or equal to the maximum values found in cells G2:G6, to be greater than or equal to the minimum values found in cells F2:F6. The three resource constraints are specified by the line giving D7:E7 as less than or equal to the limits in the block D8:E8, and cell B7 less than or equal to its limit in cell B8.

Next we can click on the Options block (Figure 8.3).

The GRG nonlinear option needs to be used if there are nonlinear functions (or even ratios that could be converted to linear) because Simplex won't linear functions. If everything is linear, as in Table 8.5,

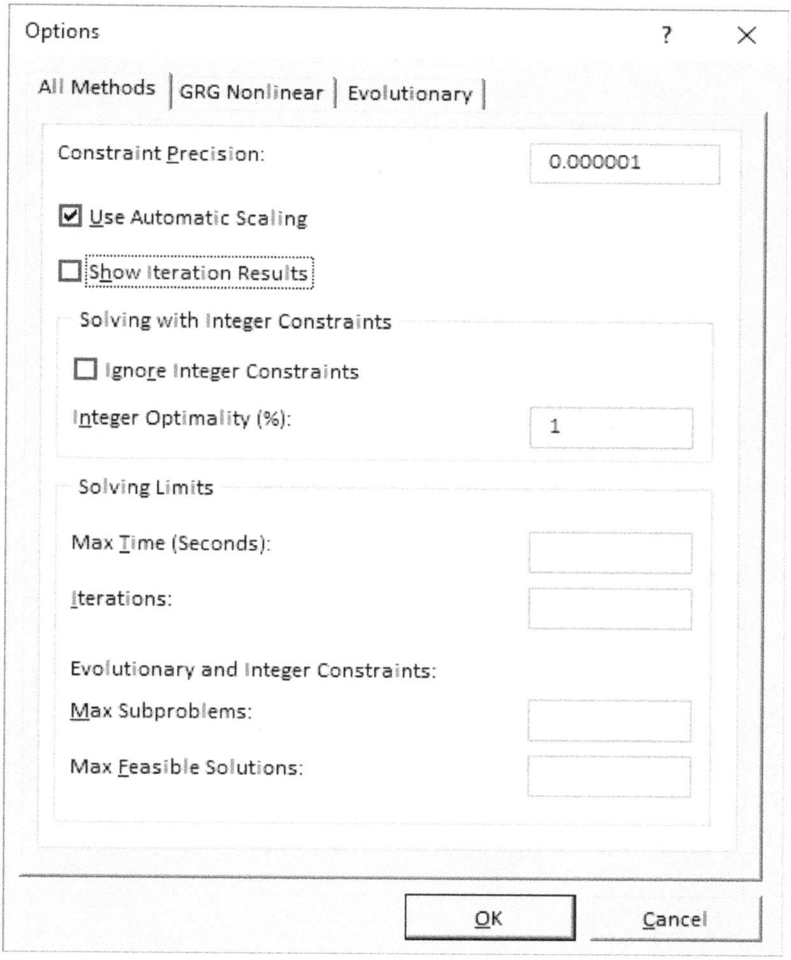

Figure 8.3 Options window

Simplex is more efficient for large scale problems, as well as avoiding rounding errors. The box to use automatic scaling should be checked, especially if some coefficients in the model are much larger than others. After entering any option we want, we click on OK, and return to the prior window. We then click on the SOLVE box. If all goes well, we will get a window saying that *Solver* found an optimal solution. The spreadsheet now looks as in Table 8.6.

The solution is to produce 5,888.9 cans of H&B, 1,000 cans of JHB, 1,000 cans of LB, 2,000 cans of JLB, and 1,000 cans of JP. This will yield a daily profit of $1,936.67. Note that the solution is not strictly feasible, because making 0.9 cans of H&B would not be useful. However, rounding down will stay within required constraints, and yield the maximum profit of over $1,936. Three products are at the specified minimums (JHB, LB, and JLB). One product is at its maximum (JP). All of the beans were used. Only 26,555 ounces of ham were used, leaving a daily surplus of 3445 ounces. The number of cans required each day will be 10,888, 13,112 below its limit.

Solver provides three output sheets. The first of these, the *answer* sheet, provides details about each variable (Table 8.7). Much of this information is found on the solved spreadsheet, such as the final objective function value of $1,936.67, and the final values for each variable. The original values in this case were all zero, as that was what the computer algorithm used as the starting point. That is unimportant for our purposes.

Table 8.6 Solver solution

	A	B	C	D	E	F	G
1	Product	Quantity	Profit	HAM	BEANS	Min	Max
2	H&B	**5,888.8889**	0.21	4	9	5,000	10,000
3	JHB	**1,000**	0.2	3	9	1,000	4,000
4	LB	**1,000**	0.1		14	1,000	6,000
5	JLB	**2,000**	0.15		12	2,000	4,000
6	JP	**1,000**	0.1			0	1,000
7	CANS	10,888.889	**1,936.6667**	26,555.55556	100,000		
8	Limits	24,000		30,000	100,000		

Table 8.7 Answer report Microsoft Excel 16.0

Objective cell (max)

Cell	Name	Original value	Final value
$C$7	CANS profit	0	1,936.666667

Variable cells

Cell	Name	Original value	Final value	Integer
$B$2	H&B quantity	0	5,888.888889	Contin
$B$3	JHB quantity	0	1,000	Contin
$B$4	LB quantity	0	1,000	Contin
$B$5	JLB quantity	0	2,000	Contin
$B$6	JP quantity	0	1,000	Contin

Constraints

Cell	Name	Cell value	Formula	Status	Slack
$B$7	CANS quantity	10,888.88889	$B$7<=$B$8	Not binding	13,111.11111
$D$7	CANS HAM	26,555.55556	$D$7<=$D$8	Not binding	3,444.444444
$E$7	CANS BEANS	100,000	$E$7<=$E$8	Binding	0
$B$2	H&B quantity	5,888.888889	$B$2<=$G$2	Not binding	4,111.111111
$B$3	JHB quantity	1,000	$B$3<=$G$3	Not binding	3,000
$B$4	LB quantity	1,000	$B$4<=$G$4	Not binding	5,000
$B$5	JLB quantity	2,000	$B$5<=$G$5	Not binding	2,000
$B$6	JP quantity	1,000	$B$6<=$G$6	Binding	0
$B$2	H&B quantity	5,888.888889	$B$2>=$F$2	Not binding	888.8888889
$B$3	JHB quantity	1,000	$B$3>=$F$3	Binding	0
$B$4	LB quantity	1,000	$B$4>=$F$4	Binding	0
$B$5	JLB quantity	2,000	$B$5>=$F$5	Binding	0
$B$6	JP quantity	1,000	$B$6>=$F$6	Not binding	1,000

Each constraint is reported, giving the cell location, its name, its final value, and its formula. Information is also provided concerning the status of the constraint, in terms of binding or not binding. **Binding** constraints are at their limits, with no slack (for ≤ constraints) or surplus (for ≥ constraints), and therefore have **Slack** of zero. Those constraints that are **Not Binding** have reported quantities of Slack, reflecting the distance of the current solution from the stated limit. For instance, the optimal solution has slightly over 3,444 ounces of ham left over from the original 30,000 ounces. (Thus, the current solution used 26,556 ounces of ham.)

In addition to the Answer Report, *Solver* makes available a Sensitivity Report sheet, and a Limits Report sheet. We will discuss these in the section on sensitivity analysis.

LP Model Assumptions

A key element of LP models is the set of assumptions required. These assumptions are **linearity, certainty**, and **continuity**. Different functions could have been selected as the objective function. The optimal solution obtained is only optimal with respect to the function used as the objective.

Linearity

All functions must be linear. Often, this is no problem. In the example problem, it seems reasonable to assume that each can will use the same quantities of materials (or very close). Quality control is applied to make sure that this happens. The function would not truly be linear, however, if there were economies of scale available. This could happen in our models with resources such as man hours, although if the decision produced by the model is not significantly different from current operations, the resulting nonlinearity should not be important. In this model, labor is represented by the function CANS. One function where nonlinearity may be a problem is the objective function of profit. If the company is large enough to be able to influence the sales price with large increases in volume, diminishing returns to scale could result. That would lead to a nonlinear profit function. Here, again, this will not be a problem if the quantity in the solution is not too large relative to current production.

Certainty

The resulting LP solution will be optimal IF the coefficients used are correct. A general LP model can be expressed:

$$\text{Maximize } \sum_{j=1}^{n} c_j x_j$$

$$\text{s.t. } \sum_{j=1}^{n} a_{ij} x_j \leq b_i \quad \text{for i=1 to m}$$

$$x_j \geq 0 \quad \text{for j=1 to n}$$

There are three classes of coefficients in this model. If contribution coefficients (c_j) are estimates, or are random variables, you will get a feasible solution, but you are not guaranteed the best possible solution. If the coefficients b_i (right-hand side values) or the technological coefficients a_{ij} are estimates with some variance, the solution may not be feasible when implemented. There is a certain degree of sensitivity analysis which can be conducted to determine how much c_j or b_i coefficients can vary before it makes any difference. There is also a limited amount of sensitivity analysis that can be accomplished if a_{ij} coefficients vary. Sensitivity analysis of a_{ij} coefficients is beyond the scope of what we want to do. The important thing to remember about certainty is that **the validity of the resulting solution depends upon the accuracy of the model coefficients**. If a coefficient varies just a bit, the resulting solution may still be useful. But a high degree of variance in coefficients invalidates the optimality of a LP solution.

Continuity

LP solutions are generally obtained with the simplex technique. That technique converts all constraints to equalities by adding slack or surplus variables. The resulting solution will be a set of variable values which simultaneously solve the entire set of equations that have the greatest (or if minimizing, the smallest) objective function value. Since the variable values are the result of simultaneously solving equations, the optimal solution may well contain fractional values. In the demonstration model, for instance, a solution of 5,888.9 cans of ham and beans was obtained. A feasible solution can usually be obtained by rounding, to either 5,888 or 5,889 cans. However, the best solution containing only integer decision variable values is not necessarily a solution with these values (in the example, it is). This can especially be a problem for variables which have to be either zero or one (for instance, do a project or don't). Sometimes, the existence of noninteger solution values does not matter. Eight days out of nine you could schedule 5,888 cans of ham and beans, and the ninth day 5,889. If it does make a difference, there are solution techniques which guarantee integer or zero-one decision variable values. (In *Solver*, simply add a constraint for B2:B6 to be INT (for integer). You can also specify variables either be 0–1 by adding a constraint for the specified variable cells to be BIN for binary, or 0–1.)

Complications

Solution of a LP model can yield a number of results. The possible results can be viewed as a tree in Figure 8.4.

The first branch is for **feasibility**. If all goes well, the model is feasible. If the constraint set includes conflicting constraints, there is no possible solution to the model. This is hopefully because one or more constraints were included that were too tight. In the canning model, if at least 8,000 cans of H&B were specified, that would be infeasible, because that would require 32,000 ounces of ham per day, and there are only 30,000 ounces available. There would additionally by a shortage of cans, as there are currently only 24,000 available. Further, there are minimum required cans of another product using ham, and other products using cans. Something would have to give. The model is feasible, with the result given.

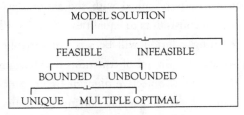

Figure 8.4 Linear programming model outcome tree

The next branch of possible model outcomes is **boundedness**. If you have a simple model with the objective of maximizing A + B subject to A ≤ 10, there is an unlimited objective function value. B could increase infinitely. An **unbounded** solution is usually due to a missing constraint, and if the computer solution indicates an unbounded solution, that is a clue to the modeler to add some missing limit to the model. The canning example is bounded, and no problem exists. In fact, all five decision variables are individually limited.

The final branch of possible outcomes is the number of optimal solutions. We would normally expect one best (**unique optimal**) solution. LP guarantees us the best objective function value to a model. There may, however, be more than one solution yielding that optimal value (**multiple optimal solutions**). Actually, multiple optimal solutions are opportunities rather than problems, because their existence would indicate more than one way to obtain the best possible outcome (as measured by the objective function). The decision maker would have added flexibility.

Additional complications: LP solution codes take care of inserting the slack/surplus variables, and obtaining the optimal solution. They work very efficiently in general, although most codes have difficulty with very large models (tens of thousands of variables and thousands of constraints). Some codes have been built to deal with over a million variables for special types of models. In general, the larger the model, the longer it takes on the computer. Also, because computers work in binary terms, rounding becomes a problem for large models. There is one potential source of severe problems, however. **Degeneracy** can occur when more than two constraints intersect at the same point. What happens is that the reduced costs/dual prices are not dependable, and the solution method could actually cycle. Most codes have been written to minimize the risk of cycling. But care must still be taken with interpretation of reduced costs/dual prices. Potential degeneracy occurs when basic variable values of 0 exist.

Sensitivity Analysis

Sensitivity analysis refers to determining how much any one coefficient could change before model results would change. We will review the major elements of sensitivity analysis, which should indicate to you how little change would be necessary to have an impact on a LP solution. That is because optimization by nature yields extreme solutions. Any change in assumed model coefficients is liable to have dramatic impact.

There are some important limits to sensitivity analysis. You can tell what will happen to the optimal solution if any model coefficient changes with the important restriction that *all* other model coefficients remain the same. If more than one coefficient were to change, more thorough techniques, such as parametric programming, would need to be applied. But that implies an enormous number of LP solutions, covering all expected coefficient value combinations. The sensitivity analysis we will discuss assumes only one coefficient change at a time. We will discuss changes in contribution rates (c_j) and right-hand side values (b_i). More advanced techniques are required to analyze the impact of changes in technological coefficients (a_{ij}).

Reduced Costs

Reduced costs are by definition the amount that a decision variable contribution coefficient must improve before that decision variable would be introduced into the solution. In effect, a reduced cost is how much a product is underpriced. For minimizations, it is how much a variable is overpriced. In the canning example, the reduced cost for H&B is zero, because this variable is in the solution, not at a limit. Three of the variables (JHB, LB, and JLB) are at their minimums, and one (JP) is at its maximum.

Solver provides a sensitivity report page providing this information (Table 8.8).

The cells containing decision variables are identified, along with name and solution value. The **Reduced Cost** column is self descriptive. Here, we see that variable JHB is at its lower limit, and has a reduced cost of −0.01. This means that adding more cans of this variable to the solution would lower the objective function by $0.01 per can, at least at the margin. The **Allowable Increase** and **Allowable Decrease** indicate the range of change in cans for which this rate applies. If the current objective coefficient for JHB were to increase by 0.01 to $0.21/can, this reduced

Table 8.8 Solver sensitivity report Microsoft 16.0

Variable cells

Cell	Name	Final value	Reduced cost	Objective coefficient	Allowable increase	Allowable decrease
$B$2	H&B quantity	5,888.888889	0	0.21	1E+30	0.01
$B$3	JHB quantity	1,000	-0.01	0.2	0.01	1E+30
$B$4	LB quantity	1,000	-0.226666667	0.1	0.226666667	1E+30
$B$5	JLB quantity	2,000	-0.13	0.15	0.13	1E+30
$B$6	JP quantity	1,000	0.1	0.1	1E+30	0.1

Constraints

Cell	Name	Final value	Shadow price	Constraint R.H. Side	Allowable increase	Allowable decrease
$B$7	CANS quantity	10,888.88889	0	24,000	1E+30	13,111.11111
$D$7	CANS HAM	26,555.5556	0	30,000	1E+30	3,444.444444
$E$7	CANS BEANS	100,000	0.023333333	100,000	7,750	8,000

cost would change. On the other hand, should this objective function coefficient drop by any amount (1E+30 is Excel's way of saying infinity), there would be no change in the current optimal solution. The variable H&B has zero reduced cost. The Allowable Increase is infinity, indicating that improving the current objective function coefficient of 0.21 by any amount would not change the optimality of the current solution. (The current solution would be more profitable, and would continue to have a better objective function value than any other feasible solution.) On the other hand, were the current H&B objective function coefficient of 0.21 per can drop by 0.01 (while all other variable objective coefficients and in fact all other model coefficients of all kinds) stayed at their current levels, there would be some other solution that would yield a superior profit. That new solution in fact, would substitute more JHB for H&B, but this new solution cannot be identified until the model is rerun with the decreased objective function coefficient for JHB. At the limit expressed by the allowable increase (a new objective function coefficient for JHB of $0.20/can), there would be multiple optimal solutions, with the current solution having a profit of $1,936.67 − (5,888.89 × −0.01) = $1,877.79, as would some other solution with less JHB.

Objective functions are not constrained. Therefore, the important feature is the relative value of contribution rates. You will get precisely the same result (decision) if you used contribution rates of cents/can as you would with dollars per can, as long as all of the contribution rates are in common terms. What matters is the relative weights, not the magnitude. Of course, the ranges and dual price information would then be in cents rather than dollars. Another implication is that if all contribution coefficients were to increase by 5% across the board, there would be no change in the optimal decision. Therefore, sensitivity analysis of contribution coefficients is only useful for change in one contribution coefficient, with the exception of the 100% rule.

The 100% rule provides a small bit of added power to determine if an optimal solution would change under conditions of **multiple** changes in contribution coefficients.

$$\text{if } \sum_{j=1}^{n} \frac{\text{change}(c_j)}{\text{allowable change}(c_j)} \leq 1, \text{ solution still optimal}$$

Table 8.9 Impact of $0.1 profit drop

Variable	Change	Allowable	Ratio
H&B	−0.1	−0.01	10
JHB	−0.1	−Infinity	0
LB	−0.1	−Infinity	0
JLB	−0.1	−Infinity	0
JP	−0.1	−0.1	1

If the sum of changes in contribution coefficients divided by their allowable changes total no more than 1.0, the 100% rule establishes that the current optimal solution would still be optimal given the changes. A tricky part is that if the sum of changes is greater than 1.0, nothing is proven. In that case, you would not know if the current solution would be the same or not.

In the example, if profit rates for all cans were all dropped $0.1, the calculation would be as shown in Table 8.9.

In this example, the sum of the ratios is greater than 1.0, and we cannot conclude that the optimal solution would remain the same. In fact, the solution would remain the same. However, the 100 percent rule would not be able to prove this.

Dual Prices

The dual prices for constraints contain a great deal of information that is highly useful.

> The definition of a dual price is **the rate of change in the objective function per unit change in right-hand side coefficient** for a particular constraint

Each constraint limits the model solution. If it weren't for a particular constraint, it is possible that the objective function would be better. There are two possibilities: the constraint is at its limit (**binding**), or the constraint is not at its limit (**nonbinding**). A nonbinding constraint has slack (for ≤ constraints) or surplus (for ≥ constraints). A nonbinding constraint

Table 8.10 Shadow price output

Constraints						
		Final	Shadow	Constraint	Allowable	Allowable
Cell	Name	Value	Price	R.H. Side	Increase	Decrease
$D$7	CANS HAM	26,555.55556	0	30,000	1E+30	3,444.444444
$E$7	CANS BEANS	100,000	0.023333333	100,000	7750	8,000
$B$7	CANS quantity	10,888.88889	0	24,000	1E+30	13,111.11111

implies that the slack/surplus variable associated with that constraint is basic. The dual price for a nonbinding constraint is by necessity zero. Because the constraint is not at its limit for the current solution, changing the right-hand side a small amount would have no impact upon the optimal solution. Therefore, the rate of change in the objective function per unit change in right-hand side would be zero. Table 8.10 shows *Solver* output for right-hand-sides.

In the ham and bean example, the constraints for ham and for cans are nonbinding. The ham constraint limits ham to 30,000 ounces, but the optimal solution only required 26,556. Thus there is a surplus of 3,444 ounces of ham. At the margin, raising (or lowering) the limit of 30,000 ounces would not change the optimal solution. The surplus variable for this constraint would decrease by 1, but the decision variables (and the objective function value) would remain the same. Therefore, the rate of change in the objective would be zero. This is indicated in the shadow price column. The same is true for the CANS quantity, as the optimal solution used 10,888.89 cans, and 24,000 were available.

If a slack/surplus constraint is binding, such as is the case for beans, the dual price gives the marginal value of that resource. If 100,001 ounces were available per day instead of 100,000, the objective function would increase by $0.0233, the dual price for beans. This implies that at the margin, an extra ounce of beans per day is worth $0.023 more than the current cost of $0.05/ounce. (The profit function is already paying $0.05/ounce.) If the firm could obtain extra beans each day at a cost of less than $0.073 per ounce, they could increase profit. On the other hand, if the firm could sell beans for more than $0.073 per ounce, the firm would be ahead to produce less product and use the beans for this more profitable activity. The dual price of $0.023 is marginal, and not average. On average, the firm is making $1,936.67 profit per day (paying $0.05/ounce for beans) for 100,000 ounces, or an average profit of $0.0019/ounce (above the $0.05/ounce paid). That is because the first beans are used for required products. Then beans are used for the most profitable product, until that most profitable product is constrained. This goes on, with ever decreasing profit/ounce of beans, until the marginal rate of $0.023/ounce (above the $0.023 cost) applies. The range analysis gives the limits in constraint right-hand side for which the current shadow price applies. The current right-hand side of 100,000 could increase by 7,750 ounces, or decrease by 8,000 ounces, before the dual price would change. This implies that between 92,250 and 108,000 ounces, each ounce contributes $0.023 to profit. Below 92,250 ounces, the marginal value would be higher. Above 108,000 ounces, the marginal value will be lower. The reason is that new combinations of constraints would limit the optimal solution at these bean levels. It should be noted that while the dual price is constant over its allowable range, the optimal solution and profit will change with each change in bean levels.

Negative dual prices occur with ≥ constraints, and possibly with strict equalities. That is because these constraints force variables into the solution, which reduces the more attractive alternatives available in the model.

In summary, there are two fundamental rules upon which all sensitivity analysis is based. Given these, you should be able to deal with a variety of questions for any kind of LP solution.

1. **Reduced costs** are the amount that a c_j must improve before it is attractive enough to be part of the basic solution (take on a nonzero value). The optimal **decision** will remain the same as long as any one c_j stays within its allowable range, and **no other model coefficients change**

2. **Dual prices** are the rate of change in the objective function per unit change in right-hand side coefficient. The **dual price** will remain constant as long as the associated b_i stays within its allowable range, and **no other model coefficients change**

Integer Models

In the discussion about the assumption of continuity, we said that simplex was liable to give fractional decision variable values in the optimal solution. For some models, this is unacceptable. For instance, you cannot physically have 0.48 of a building, or buy 0.85 automobiles.

There is absolutely no problem modeling those cases where integer or zero-one restrictions on the variables are required. Simply specify variables by the appropriate class, and add these specifications to the model. There **is** a problem **solving** these classes of models.

Excel's Solver takes care of all of this logic. All that you have to do to obtain an integer solution is to constrain the selected variables to be INT (for integer), as demonstrated in Figure 8.5.

This yields the solution in Table 8.11.

Variables can also be specified as BIN (binary, or 0–1).

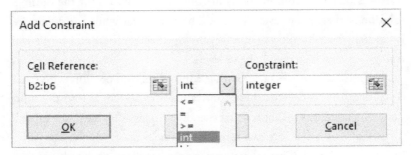

Figure 8.5 Adding integer restriction in Solver

Table 8.11 Integer solution

	A	B	C	D	E	F
1	Product	Quantity	Profit	HAM	BEANS	Min
2	H&B	5,888	0.21	4	9	5,000
3	JHB	1,000	0.2	3	9	1,000
4	LB	1,000	0.1		14	1,000
5	JLB	2,000	0.15		12	2,000
6	JP	1,000	0.1			0
7	CANS	10,888	1,936.48	26,552	99,992	
8	Limits	24,000		30,000	100,000	

Zero-One Programming

Zero-one variables are very useful in a number of operations management contexts, such as plant scheduling (where machine setups are required between production runs for different products) and inventory models (where orders are placed with a cost independent of order quantity).

We will demonstrate the latter problem with a case where a manufacturer produces a unique laundry detergent to customer order quantities. Demand is set over the next month by orders from a short list of clientele. Materials for the soap are developed locally, except for a specialty liquid cleanser additive delivered by tanker (which, due to the special chemical properties of this additive, charges $5,000 per delivery, no matter what quantity is ordered). This liquid additive is expensive to inventory, and costs the manufacturer $5 per gallon per week to store. Each case (144 boxes) of soap uses up 0.1 gallons of additive.

The decision here is how much additive to order by time period. Problem features are as in Table 8.12.

One option is to order what is needed each week. This would minimize inventory holding costs, but would involve four orders. The total quantity of additive required over the four week planning horizon is 6,000 gallons, which could be ordered to arrive at the beginning of week one, minimizing ordering costs. But mathematical programming can provide an optimal solution over the current planning horizon minimizing the sum of holding and ordering costs. (After one week of operation, the model can be rerun with a new fifth week of data.)

Objective

The decision is to minimize total inventory cost. In this case, this is independent of production cost, and independent of purchasing cost, although both factors could play a role and could be included in the

Table 8.12 Zero-one model parameters

	Week 1	Week 2	Week 3	Week 4
Demand (cases soap)	10,000	20,000	5,000	25,000
Additive required/week	1,000 gal	2,000 gal	500 gal	2,500 gal

model. The inventory factors of importance here are ordering costs ($5,000 per order) and holding costs ($5 per gallon per week of inventory carried over from one week to the next). Holding costs within the week delivered are not a factor, as they would be incurred regardless of policy.

Combining holding costs with ordering costs, the objective function would be:

Minimize 5 C12 + 5 C23 + 5 C34 + 5000 Y1 + 5000 Y2 + 5000 Y3 + 5000 Y4

Variables

The decision variables reflect the quantity to be ordered by week. We can reflect this by four variables, X1 through X4, numbered by the week of receipt (delivery assumed at the beginning of each week). We also need variables to reflect the costs incurred. We need variables to represent orders (Y1 through Y4), again numbered by week of delivery. We also need variables reflecting inventory carryover (C12, C23, and C34) where the number reflects the beginning week and the second number the week to which inventory is carried over to.

Constraints

We need to model balance constraints reflecting the possible sources of additive for each week. For week 1, there is only one source: delivery at the beginning of week 1. But for subsequent weeks, multiple sources are possible (and if there was an initial quantity on hand, it could be used for week one as well). For each week:

Carried over from week n − 1 + Purchased week n = Used week n + Carried over to week n + 1

For the specific model:

Week 1		X1	=	1,000	+ C12
Week 2	C12 +	X2	=	2,000	+ C23
Week 3	C23 +	X3	=	500	+ C34
Week 4	C34 +	X4	=	2,500	(+ C45)

Note that we do not have an initial inventory, nor do we model past the current planning horizon, so for our model, C45 will be zero.

We also need constraints to reflect the relationship between quantities purchased and orders placed. We can take advantage of the zero-one variables Y1 through Y4 to apply logic. These four variables are used in the objective function to incur costs of ordering.

The constraint set required to trigger orders would be:

X1	$\leq$	9,999 Y1
X2	$\leq$	9,999 Y2
X3	$\leq$	9,999 Y3
X4	$\leq$	9,999 Y4

Here the value 9,999 is used to reflect a number guaranteed to be larger than the maximum value of Xn. In this case, Xn could be as high as 6,000. We need a number that in general is expected to be well above the maximum value for Xn. The logic is that if any quantity is received in a period, a delivery is incurred.

The EXCEL model is given in Table 8.13.

In columns C through K of the function row (row 14), sum products were used. For column C:

$$=SUMPRODUCT(\$B\$2:\$B\$12,C2:C12)$$

This was copied across through column K, identifying function values for each column. The *Solver* input is shown in Figure 8.6.

Each of the eight continuous variables was restricted to be non-negative. The four zero-one variables were specified as binary (zero or one). The four structural equalities modeling the carryover variables are imposed by the constraints:

$$\$D\$14:\$G\$14=\$D\$13:\$D\$13$$

Finally, the four trigger constraints for the zero-one variables are modeled:

$$\$H\$14:\$K\$14 <= 0$$

The solution obtained indicates orders placed in weeks one, two, and four. Therefore, three ordering costs were incurred, resulting in $15,000

Table 8.13 Excel zero-one model

	A	B	C	D	E	F	G	H	I	J	K
1		Variables	Costs	Week 1	Week 2	Week 3	Week 4	Trigger 1	Trigger 2	Trigger 3	Trigger 4
2	x1	1,000		1				1			
3	x2	2,500			1				1		
4	x3	0				1				1	
5	x4	2,500					1				1
6	c12	0	5	−1	1						
7	c23	500	5		−1	1					
8	c34	0	5			−1	1				
9	y1	1	5,000					−9,999			
10	y2	1	5,000						−9,999		
11	y3	0	5,000							−9,999	
12	y4	1	5,000								−9,999
13	use			1,000	2,000	500	2,500	0	0	0	0
14	function		17,500	1,000	2,000	500	2,500	−8,999	−7,499	−0	−7,499

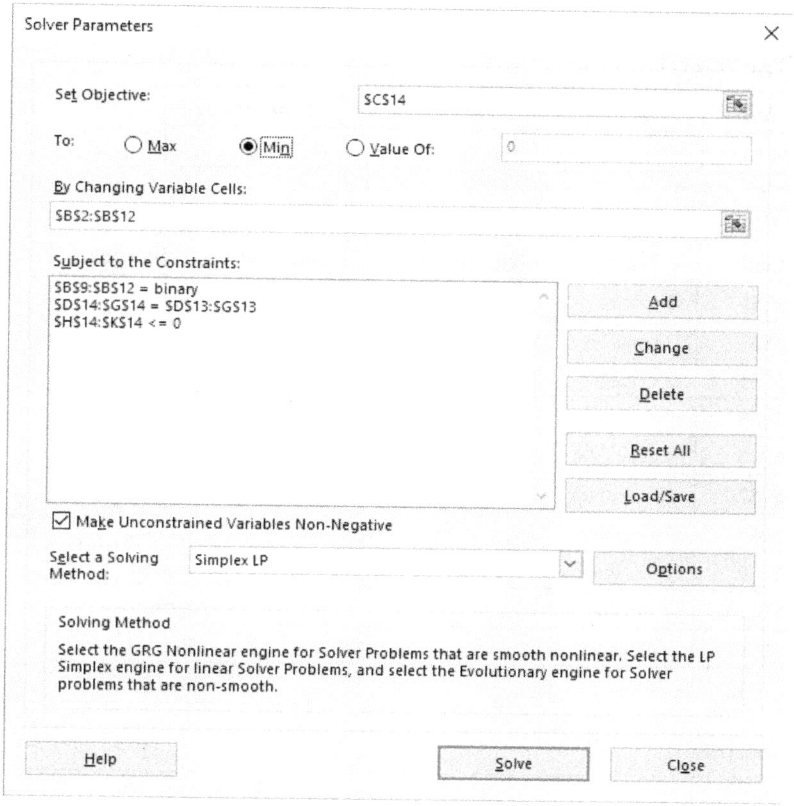

Figure 8.6 Zero-one Solver input

of expense. Holding costs were incurred from week two to week three, for a quantity of 500 units at $5 per unit, or $2,500. This yields the total expense of $17,500. The Answer Sheet provided by *Solver* is Table 8.14.

The constraint report indicates which constraints are binding, and their slack. However, this information is not as useful as it was in the continuous model case. Note that when zero-one or integer variables are used, sensitivity analysis is unreliable (because a number of additional constraints are generated by the computer internally to identify the optimal zero-one or integer solution). *Solver* does not provide sensitivity analysis when zero-one or integer variables are present.

The solution obtained to the zero-one model compares favorably with both extreme solutions. Ordering each week would have no holding costs, but would have 4 × $5,000 = $20,000 in ordering costs. Making one

Table 8.14 Solver zero-one answer Microsoft 16.0

Objective cell (min)

Cell	Name	Original value	Final value
$C$14	Function costs	17,500	17,500

Variable cells

Cell	Name	Original value	Final value	Integer
$B$2	x1 variables	1,000	1,000	Contin
$B$3	x2 variables	2,500	2,500	Contin
$B$4	x3 variables	0	0	Contin
$B$5	x4 variables	2,500	2,500	Contin
$B$6	c12 variables	0	0	Contin
$B$7	c23 variables	500	500	Contin
$B$8	c34 variables	0	0	Contin
$B$9	y1 variables	1	1	Binary
$B$10	y2 variables	1	1	Binary
$B$11	y3 variables	0	0	Binary
$B$12	y4 variables	1	1	Binary

Constraints

Cell	Name	Cell value	Formula	Status	Slack
$D$14	Function week 1	1,000	$D$14=$D$13	Binding	0
$E$14	Function week 2	2,000	$E$14=$E$13	Binding	0
$F$14	Function week 3	500	$F$14=$F$13	Binding	0
$G$14	Function week 4	2,500	$G$14=$G$13	Binding	0
$H$14	Function trigger 1	–8,999	$H$14<=0	Not Binding	8,999
$I$14	Function trigger 2	–7,499	$I$14<=0	Not Binding	7,499
$J$14	Function trigger 3	0	$J$14<=0	Binding	0
$K$14	Function trigger 4	–7,499	$K$14<=0	Not Binding	7,499
$B$9:$B$12=Binary					

initial order would only have $5,000 in ordering costs, but would involve inventory costs of 5,000 × $5 from week one to week two (25,000), 3,000 × $5 from week two to week three ($15,000), and 2,500 × $5 from week three to week four ($12,500), or a whopping $52,500 in holding costs.

Zero-one models can be used for a number of interesting applications, some of which are very important in operations management. For instance, production line scheduling involving machine setups is commonly modeled with zero-one variables for setups.

Transportation Models

Transportation models are concerned with cases where materials need to be moved from source locations to demand locations. Each combination of source to demand is a variable. If some combination is infeasible, this combination can be eliminated from the variable set. The cost per unit of material for of each combination of source and demand is reflected in the objective function, which is typically to minimize cost.

For example, an automobile manufacturer may have a number of factories capable of producing a given vehicle model. A set of possible factory locations is given in the following. This manufacturing process may require engines, which could be obtained from a variety of sources. Say that the manufacturer has an engine production facility in Dearborn, MI, and another in Scottsdale, AZ. They could also import engines from Japan. Model parameters are given in Table 8.15.

The model includes a variable for each combination of Source and Demand (twelve in all). Each of these variables has a unit cost, given in the following table, here representing price FOB plant (purchase plus shipping). We will represent each variable by the initial of the Source, combined with the initial of the Demand. The objective is to minimize the total cost function:

Table 8.15 Transportation model parameters

Unit costs	Sources			Required/week
Demands	Dearborn	Scottsdale	Japan	
Reno	80	20	160	1,600
Waco	70	30	170	1,700
Xenia	30	70	190	1,900
Macon	50	80	200	2,000
Available	2,000	3,000	8,000	

Min 80 DR + 20 SR + 160 JR + 70 DW + 30 SW + 170 JW + 30 DX
+ 70 SX + 190 JX + 50 DM + 80 SM + 200 JM

There are constraints required to make sure that supply quantities at each Source are not exceeded, and that the sum provided to each Demand is at least the quantity needed. We can use equalities if the total supply exactly matches the total demand. More generally, as is the case here, it is wiser to leave constraints in their less restricted form (inequalities).

Source limits		Demand requirements
DR + DW + DX + DM	≤ 2000	DR + SR + JR ≥ 1600
SR + SW + SX + SM	≤ 3000	DR + SR + JR ≥ 1700
JR + JW + JX + JM	≤ 8000	DR + SR + JR ≥ 1900
		DR + SR + JR ≥ 2000

We also need to restrict each of the 12 individual variables to be greater than or equal to zero. The EXCEL model is shown in Table 8.16.

The *Solver* input to reflect this model is shown in Figure 8.7.

The *solver* solution for this model is in Table 8.17.

It will take over $500 thousand per time period to ship the required engines. The Scottsdale source is assigned to the Reno and Waco plants, and the surplus requirements at Reno obtained from Japan. The Dearborn source is dedicated to the Xenia and Durham plant, and again surplus requirements at Durham obtained from Japan. The solution requires 2,200 engines per time period from Japan. Here, the supply-demand combinations with minimum cost were applied, and Japanese resources used for the remainder of the solution.

Assignment Models

The assignment model is a special case of the transportation model. While the quantities demanded and supplied in a transportation model can be any value, these quantities are one in the assignment model.

A prototypical example is assigning personnel to tasks. We all have some things that we do very well, and other things that we would rather not do. Fortunately, we all do not like or dislike the same things. Consider an office with four new workers, and four job classifications. After the

Table 8.16 Excel transportation model

	A	B	C	D	E	F
1	Unit costs	Sources			Total cost	
2	Demands	Dearborn	Scottsdale	Japan		
3	Reno	80	20	160		
4	Waco	70	30	170		
5	Xenia	30	70	190		
6	Durham	50	80	200		
7					=SUMPRODUCT(B3:D6,B10:D13)	
8	Variables					
9	Demands	Dearborn	Scottsdale	Japan	Total	At least
10	Reno				=SUM(B10:D10)	1,600
11	Waco				=SUM(B11:D11)	1,700
12	Xenia				=SUM(B12:D12)	1,900
13	Durham				=SUM(B13:D13)	2,000
14	Total	=SUM(B10:B13)	=SUM(C10:C13)	=SUM(D10:D13)	=SUM(E10:E13)	
15	No more than	2,000	3,000	8,000		

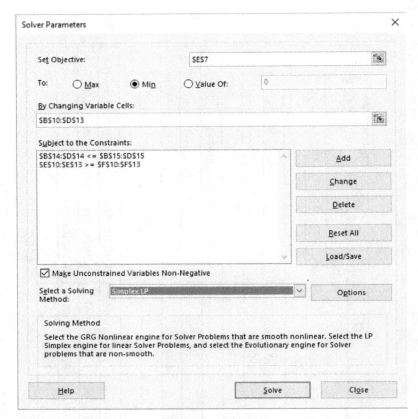

Figure 8.7 Solver transportation model input

Table 8.17 Transportation model solution

Unit costs	Sources			Total cost	
Demands	Dearborn	Scottsdale	Japan		
Reno	80	20	160		
Waco	70	30	170		
Xenia	30	70	190		
Durham	50	80	200		
				567,000	
Variables					
Demands	Dearborn	Scottsdale	Japan	Total	At least
Reno	0	1,300	300	1,600	1,600

Waco	0	1,700	0	1,700	1,700
Xenia	1,900	0	0	1,900	1,900
Durham	100	0	1,900	2,000	2,000
Total	2,000	3,000	2,200	7,200	
No more than	2,000	3,000	8,000		

Table 8.18 Assignment model parameters

	Accounting	Finance reports	Shipping schedules	Stock trades
Jay Gould	3 hours	4 hours	3 hours	1 hour
John P. Morgan	5 hours	2 hours	6 hours	4 hours
John Rockefeller	1 hour	7 hours	4 hours	6 hours
Cornelius Vanderbilt	4 hours	9 hours	2 hours	2 hours

initial training period, the human resources staff has measured the average time for each to accomplish a typical task in four areas of work processed in the office. Model parameters are given in Table 8.18.

This problem can be modeled in LP as follows:

Min 3 GA + 4 GF + 3 GS + 1 GT + 5 MA + 2 MF + 6 MS + 4 MT + 1 RA + 7 RF + 4 RS + 6 RT + 4 VA + 9 VF + 2 VS + 2 VT

Subject to: GA + GF + GS + GT = 1 Each person assigned exactly once

MA + MF + MS + MT = 1
RA + RF + RS + RT = 1
VA + VF + VS + VT = 1
GA + MA + RA + VA = 1   Each task assigned to one person
GF + MF + RF + VF = 1
GS + MS + RS + VS = 1
GT + MT + RT + VT = 1

All variables greater than or equal to one (in fact, binary).

The Excel model is shown in Table 8.19.

The solution to this model is indicated by the "1"s in the variable section. The result is given in Table 8.20.

Table 8.19 *Excel assignment model*

	A	B	C	D	E	F
1		Accounting	Finance	Shipping	Stock	
2	Gould	3	4	3	1	
3	Morgan	3	5	6	3	
4	Rockefeller	1	7	4	4	
5	Vanderbilt	3	6	2	3	
6						
7	Gould	0	0	0	1	=SUM(B7:E7)
8	Morgan	0	1	0	0	=SUM(B8:E8)
9	Rockefeller	1	0	0	0	=SUM(B9:E9)
10	Vanderbilt	0	0	1	0	=SUM(B10:E10)
11		=SUM(B7:B10)	=SUM(C7:C10)	=SUM(D7:D10)	=SUM(E7:E10)	
12				Total cost	=SUMPRODUCT(B2:E5,B7:E10)	

Table 8.20 Assignment model assignments

Jay Gould	Stock trades	1 hour average
John Morgan	Finance reports	5 hour average
John Rockefeller	Accounting	1 hour average
Cornelius Vanderbilt	Shipping schedules	3 hour average

Assignment models are much easier to solve than transportation models (and in fact can be solved manually quite easily), but have far fewer and less important applications. Still, there are occasions where the assignment model is useful in operations management.

Summary

LP is one of the most powerful analytic tools available for decision support systems. LP provides a means to generate solutions with the model that are optimal for the given objective function. Not only is the best possible decision (relative to the objective function) promised, but also economic interpretation of the limits to the decision is available. However, the conclusions to be drawn from LP are highly sensitive to the accuracy of the model. Errors in data, or changes in demands, costs, or resource usage, can make major differences. This is because by definition, LP seeks the very best possible solution, squeezing the last bit of objective function value from the constraint set. Thus, while LP is extremely attractive, it is extremely dangerous. And the assumptions required are more difficult to satisfy.

We covered quite a few variants of LP models, but there are more. Nonlinear models can be solved with the GRG variant of *Solver*, for instance. The basic fundamental concept of optimization is key to business analytics—the ideal sought for when modeling. Unfortunately, not all of the problems in business allow the assumptions required for optimization models.

It is often useful to use the R system, which includes support for LP. We find Solver provides the support needed, but there is additional support available, to include the free online book: http://omniascience.com/scholar/index.php/scholar/article/view/20/15

CHAPTER 9

Business Analytic Modeling Tools

This book began with discussion of general business decision making, knowledge management, and views of business analytics. Business analytics is not only about quantitative modeling—it includes consideration of data, management information systems, and acquisition of all forms of knowledge needed by businesses, to include tacit (undocumented; unspoken; implicit but not well-defined) knowledge. This book has focused on modeling tools as means to implementing business analytics in various important business decision contexts. We will conclude with an overview of the era of big data, data mining, and a review of the business analytic modeling tools we have covered in prior chapters.

The Era of Big Data

Our society has linked all of us in many ways, generating massive quantities of data from social media, the Internet of things, and many other sources. Data mining refers to the analysis of large quantities of data that are stored in computers. Bar coding has made checkout very convenient for us and provides retail establishments with masses of data. Grocery stores and other retail stores are able to quickly process our purchases and use computers to accurately determine the product prices. These same computers can help the stores with their inventory management, by instantaneously determining the quantity of items of each product on hand. Computers allow the store's accounting system to more accurately measure costs and determine the profit that store stockholders are concerned about. All of this information is available based on the bar coding information attached to each product. Along with many other sources of information, information gathered through bar coding can be used for data mining analysis.

The era of big data in here, with many sources pointing out that more data are created over the past year or two than was generated throughout all prior human history. Big data involves datasets so large that traditional data analytic methods no longer work due to data volume. Big data is often described as:

- Data too big to fit on a single server
- Data too unstructured to fit in a row-and-column database
- Data flowing too continuously to fit into a static data warehouse
- Lack of structure is the most important aspect (even more than the size)
- The point is to *analyze*, converting data into insights, innovation, and business value

The era of big data is expected to emphasize focusing on knowing what (based on correlation) rather than the traditional obsession for causality. The emphasis will be on discovering patterns offering novel and useful insights. Data will become a raw material for business, a vital economic input and source of value. Some new characteristics of this data include:

1. There is so much data available that sampling is usually not needed (*n*=all).
2. Precise accuracy of data is, thus, less important as inevitable errors are compensated for by the mass of data (any one observation is flooded by others).
3. Correlation is more important than causality—most data mining applications involving big data are interested in what is going to happen, and you don't need to know why.

Automatic trading programs need to detect the trend changes, not figure out that the Greek economy collapsed or the Chinese government will devalue the Renminbi (RMB). The programs in vehicles need to detect that an axle bearing is getting hot and the vehicle is vibrating and the wheel should be replaced, not whether this is due to a bearing failure or a housing rusting out.

There are many sources of big data. Internal to the corporation, e-mails, blogs, enterprise systems, and automation lead to structured, unstructured, and semistructured information within the organization. External data is also widely available, much of it free over the Internet, but much also available from the commercial vendors. There also is data obtainable from social media.

Data Mining

Data mining is not limited to business. Both major parties in the U.S. elections utilize data mining of potential voters. Data mining has been heavily used in the medical field, from diagnosis of patient records to help identify the best practices. Business use of data mining is also impressive. Toyota used data mining of its data warehouse to determine more efficient transportation routes, reducing the time to deliver cars to their customers by an average 19 days. Data warehouses are very large scale database systems capable of systematically storing all transactional data generated by a business organization, such as Walmart. Toyota also was able to identify the sales trends faster and to identify the best locations for new dealerships.

Data mining is widely used by banking firms in soliciting credit card customers, by insurance and telecommunication companies in detecting fraud, by manufacturing firms in quality control, and many other applications. Data mining is being applied to improve food product safety, criminal detection, and tourism. *Micromarketing* targets small groups of highly responsive customers. Data on consumer and lifestyle data is widely available, enabling customized individual marketing campaigns. This is enabled by *customer profiling*, identifying those subsets of customers most likely to be profitable to the business, as well as **targeting**, determining the characteristics of the most profitable customers.

Data mining involves statistical and artificial intelligence (AI) analysis, usually applied to large-scale datasets. There are two general types of data mining studies. *Hypothesis testing* involves expressing a theory about the relationship between actions and outcomes. This approach is referred to as *supervised*. In a simple form, it can be hypothesized that advertising will yield greater profit. This relationship has long been studied by retailing firms in the context of their specific operations. Data mining is applied to identifying relationships based on large quantities of data, which could include testing the response rates to various types of advertising on the sales and profitability of specific product lines. However, there is more to data mining than the technical tools used. The second form of data mining study is *knowledge discovery*. Data mining involves a spirit of knowledge discovery (learning new and useful things). Knowledge discovery is referred to as *unsupervised*. In this form of analysis, a preconceived notion may not be present, but rather relationships can be identified by looking at the data. This may be supported by visualization tools, which display data, or through fundamental statistical analysis, such as correlation analysis. Much of this can be accomplished through automatic means, as we will see in decision tree analysis, for example. But data mining is not limited to automated analysis. Knowledge discovery by humans can be enhanced by graphical tools and identification of unexpected patterns through a combination of human and computer interaction.

Business Analytics Modeling

Management science is the application of scientific approaches to managerial decision problems. These models apply mathematics to enable decision makers or analysts to experiment with decision components, ideally seeking optimal decisions. Management science models play a role in the broader field of knowledge management.

Knowledge management seeks to put what humans observe into context, using the information obtained to try to identify patterns or cause-and-effect relationships between actions business decision makers can take and their intended results. By trying to be systematic and objective, humans seek to gain understanding, and identify better results from their decision making.

The rational management decision process seeks to identify the system of relationships in business operations, trying to be as scientific as possible in order to objectively improve operations. A rational decision process might include:

- Defining the decision problem, or need to take action
  (identify the mission)

- Search for data and/or solutions (management information systems are one source)
- Generate alternative means to accomplish the mission
- Analyze (it is here that the models presented in this book might be applied)
- Select action
- Implement the action selected

Note that modeling is by no means the entire story. The models we have presented are only tools that can support efforts to make better decisions.

Model Classification

We can conclude with a classification of the tools that we have discussed. Table 9.1 lists a broad classification, with general function for each modeling type.

After an initial discussion of knowledge management in Chapter 1, this book discussed some visualization tools in Chapter 2. These tools are important in gaining personal understanding, as well as in communicating to others in the organization, seeking a shared basis for coordinated efforts. Chapters 3 and 4 covered some fundamental statistical tools that have been used to monitor operations quality, as well as generally

Table 9.1 Business analytic modeling tool classification

Model type	Function	Book coverage
Visualization	Describe	Chapter 2
Statistics	Measure	Chapters 3 and 4
Probabilistic analysis	Problems with distributions	Other books—analytic models such as queuing analysis
Forecasting	Prediction	Chapter 5
Multiple regression	Cause-and-effect	Chapter 6
Logistic regression	Classification—data mining	Chapter 7
Simulation	Risk	Other books—risk management
Optimization	Identify best solution	Chapter 8
Game theory	Competitive environments	Other books

support formal testing of hypotheses. Not all modeling tools were covered in the book by any means. There is an entire field of useful probabilistic analytic models such as queuing theory, Markov chains, and other tools that utilize distributions of data. Regression was covered in Chapters 5 through 7. Chapter 5 covered simple regression, focusing on time series forecasting. Chapter 6 covered multiple regression, useful in analyzing cause-and-effect relationships. Logistic regression in Chapter 7 is a fundamental tool used in data mining, where many problems involve dealing with classification of dependent variables into discrete groups. Related to probabilistic analysis is simulation, where instead of analytic models, numerical analysis based on random number streams are widely used for problems involving probability distributions. This book does not have the space to cover either of these interesting and useful tools. But the ideal goal of optimization was covered in Chapter 8, at least with the simpler version of linear programming models. There are more complex forms of optimization models not covered. Another type of model not covered is game theory, which tries to analyze competitive environments where the actions of others affect the optimality of solutions.

Thus we admit that we have not covered all models, nor have we covered all that is important in knowledge management. But we have covered some useful analytic tools that can be applied to aid the overall decision process in business.

References

Davenport, T. H. 2013. *Analytics 3.0*. Boston: Harvard Business Review Press.

Davenport, T. H. 2014. *Big Data at Work*. Boston: Harvard Business Review Press.

Rothberg, H. N., G. S. Erickson. 2005. *From Knowledge to Intelligence: Creating Competitive Advantage in the Next Economy*. Woburn, MA: Elsevier Butterworth-Heinemann.

About the Authors

Majid Nabavi has published in *Quality Management Journal,* and presented research in regional and national conferences. His teaching areas include operations management, management science, database systems, and business analytics.

David L. Olson has published research in over 150 refereed journal articles, primarily on the topic of multiple objective decision making and information technology. He teaches in the management information systems, management science, and operations management areas. He has authored over 20 books. He is associate editor of *Decision Support Systems, International Journal of Production Research,* and *Decision Sciences* and co-editor in chief of *International Journal of Services Sciences.* He has made over 200 presentations at international and national conferences on research topics. He is a member of the Decision Sciences Institute, the Institute for Operations Research and Management Sciences, and the Multiple Criteria Decision Making Society. He was named the Raymond E. Miles Distinguished Scholar award for 2002, and was a James C. and Rhonda Seacrest Fellow from 2005 to 2006. He was named Best Enterprise Information Systems Educator by IFIP in 2006. He is a Fellow of the Decision Sciences Institute.

Index

OTHER TITLES IN OUR BIG DATA AND BUSINESS ANALYTICS COLLECTION

Mark Ferguson, University of South Carolina, Editor

- *Business Intelligence and Data Mining* by Anil Maheshwari
- *Data Mining Models* by David L. Olson
- *Big Data War: How to Survive Global Big Data Competition* by Patrick Park
- *Analytics Boot Camp: Basic Analytics for Business Students and Professionals* by Linda Herkenhoff and John Fogli
- *Location Analytics for Business: The Research and Marketing Strategic Advantage* by David Z. Beitz
- *Business Analytics: A Data-Driven Decision Making Approach for Business, Volume I* by Amar Sahay

Announcing the Business Expert Press Digital Library

Concise e-books business students need for classroom and research

This book can also be purchased in an e-book collection by your library as

- a one-time purchase,
- that is owned forever,
- allows for simultaneous readers,
- has no restrictions on printing, and
- can be downloaded as PDFs from within the library community.

Our digital library collections are a great solution to beat the rising cost of textbooks. E-books can be loaded into their course management systems or onto students' e-book readers.
The **Business Expert Press** digital libraries are very affordable, with no obligation to buy in future years. For more information, please visit **www.businessexpertpress.com/librarians**. To set up a trial in the United States, please email **sales@businessexpertpress.com**.

CPSIA information can be obtained
at www.ICGtesting.com
Printed in the USA
FSHW020912021219

9 781949 443271